W9-AVD-108

LIGHT
BEFORE
THE
SON

OLD TESTAMENT STORIES OF JESUS

NAVPRESS

Bringing Truth to Life
P.O. Box 35001, Colorado Springs, Colorado 80935

OUR GUARANTEE TO YOU

We believe so strongly in the message of our books that we are making this quality guarantee to you. If for any reason you are disappointed with the content of this book, return the title page to us with your name and address and we will refund to you the list price of the book. To help us serve you better, please briefly describe why you were disappointed. Mail your refund request to: NavPress, P.O. Box 35002, Colorado Springs, CO 80935.

The Navigators is an international Christian organization. Our mission is to reach, disciple, and equip people to know Christ and to make Him known through successive generations. We envision multitudes of diverse people in the United States and every other nation who have a passionate love for Christ, live a lifestyle of sharing Christ's love, and multiply spiritual laborers among those without Christ.

NavPress is the publishing ministry of The Navigators. NavPress publications help believers learn biblical truth and apply what they learn to their lives and ministries. Our mission is to stimulate spiritual formation among our readers.

www.navpress.com
Library of Congress Catalog Card Number: 2001044738
ISBN 1-57683-279-1

Cover design by Ray Moore
Cover illustration by PhotoDisc
Creative Team: Toben Heim, Lisa Brock, Greg Clouse, Amy Spencer, Pat Miller

Some of the anecdotal illustrations in this book are true to life and are included with the permission of the persons involved. All other illustrations are composites of real situations, and any resemblance to people living or dead is coincidental.

Unless otherwise identified, all Scripture quotations in this publication are taken from the *HOLY BIBLE: NEW INTERNATIONAL VERSION*® (NIV®). Copyright © 1973, 1978, 1984 by International Bible Society. Used by permission of Zondervan Publishing House. All rights reserved. Other versions used include the *New King James Version* (NKJV). Copyright © 1982 by Thomas Nelson, Inc. Used by permission. All rights reserved. And the *Holy Bible, New Living Translation* (NLT) copyright © 1996. Used by permission of Tyndale House Publishers, Inc., Wheaton, Illinois 60189. All rights reserved.

Treadwell, Julianna
    Light before the sone: Old Testament stories of Jesus / Julianna Treadwell.
        p. cm.
    Includes bibliographical references.
    ISBN 1-57683-279-1 (hc.)
        1. Typology (Theology) I. Title

    BT225 .T67 2002
    221.6'4--dc21

                                                                                    2001044738

Printed in the United States of America

1 2 3 4 5 6 7 8 9 10 / 06 05 04 03 02

FOR A FREE CATALOG OF
NAVPRESS BOOKS & BIBLE STUDIES,
CALL 1-800-366-7788 (USA)
OR 1-416-499-4615 (CANADA)

To Steve Treadwell—my husband, my gift.
To Stan and Ruth Ann Brase—my parents, my blessing.
Thank you for giving so much to my life.
I've poured it into these pages.

CONTENTS

ACKNOWLEDGMENTS

How thankful I am for those who have touched my soul:

My sister, Jill Griffin: When this book was only an idea, you caught the vision for it. You'll never know how many times I've thought about your words of encouragement.

My friend, Kerri Ely: God's little agent! Your excitement and support have blessed me so much. Above the clatter of my computer keyboard, I've always heard your cheers and applause.

Director of Sales and Marketing Toben Heim: Thank you for taking this project under your wing. You have given my writing a place to live—in a real book!

My editor, Lisa Brock: How your fingerprints have graced this book! Thank you for being such a kind guide.

Senior Developmental Editor, Greg Clouse, Author Relations Coordinator Nanci McAlister, Creative Department Manager Ray Moore, and all the staff at NavPress: To work with you has been a dream come true. Thank you for all you've done.

My friends, Maureen Sabin, Kelly Crowther, Raquel Petersen: Your love and prayers have enriched my life. Thank you for always refilling me with your laughter.

My friend, Laurie Geisz: Such incredible blessings have come to this book through your hands! My heart will always be warmed by your dedication.

Our Italy buddies, Wes and Elin Headrick: Your

enthusiasm for this book has been such a motivation to me. Thank you for good food, good conversation, and great friendship.

My father- and mother-in-law, Richard and Sharon Treadwell: You have not only blessed me by raising such an amazing son, but by being such wonderful in-laws. Thank you for all of your support.

My childhood shepherds, Paul and Phyllis Stanley: How often has God heard you say my name? Countless times, I know. Your prayers and love have been a foundation for my life. I would not be the same without you.

My Rock and Redeemer and Restorer, God: I love You, and I love writing with You. Thank You for holding my hand and placing my feet on solid ground.

ON THE
ROAD

I kicked a small rock to the other side of the dusty road and watched it roll to a stop.

"How could Jesus have gotten out of that tomb?" I heard Cleopas mumble.

"I don't know," his friend said, glancing over his shoulder at me and then turning back around. "But Mary said He's alive."

"No one can move a stone that big," Cleopas said.

He's right, I thought, feeling my heart sink.

"What do you think?" Cleopas called to me.

I shrugged. My throat felt so tight I could barely breathe. It was like I had died with Jesus. Everything I believed in was gone.

"Well," Cleopas said, facing forward again, "I'm glad we're getting out of Jerusalem. It's easier to talk about Jesus without the Pharisees around."

Maybe, I thought.

But I was leaving to get away from Golgotha. How could I look at that bloody place again? Certainly, spending time in the town of Emmaus would clear my mind. I always liked visiting my friends who lived in the small village.

"It's a beautiful day," a voice called from behind us.

I turned around to see a man walking up the road.

"It's good to be alive," he said, smiling.

He looked at the sky and took a deep breath.

How can he be so happy? Can't he see that we're in despair?

"I've never seen people walk so slowly," he went on. "You must be discussing something interesting."[1]

Of course, I thought. *Everyone's talking about the crucifixion.*

"Are you just a visitor to Jerusalem?" Cleopas said to the stranger. "Don't you know about Jesus?"[2]

"Jesus?"

"Yes," Cleopas said, "He was just executed."

I couldn't talk about it anymore. "Excuse me," I said, stepping over the stranger's feet. "I think I'll be on my way."

There was no reason to stay. I wasn't traveling with Cleopas, anyway. We just happened to meet on the road.

"Maybe I'll see you in Emmaus," I said, walking past them.

Cleopas never looked at me.

"Don't you know that Jesus was crucified and buried?" he continued, staring at the man. "Some people say that He's alive, but we haven't seen Him."[3]

My whole body ached as I again kicked the rock and continued down the road.

"How foolish you are," the stranger said.

I quickly stopped.

"Why haven't you believed what the prophets have spoken?" he asked.[4]

Prophets? I thought. *What did the prophets say?*

"Didn't Christ have to suffer these things and then enter His glory?"[5] the stranger went on. "Moses explained it all. So did the Prophets."[6]

But I had read their writings. They never said anything about the crucifixion.

"Come with me," the man said, motioning down the road. "Let me tell you what the ancient Scriptures say about Jesus."

❧

I would have walked for miles with Jesus, if only I was really there on the road to Emmaus. I would have listened for hours as the crucified and risen Christ explained who He was by using the Old Testament.

But what did He say? How could He have taught about Himself from such empty chapters? The name of Jesus is *never* mentioned in the Old Testament. Aren't the pages just full of facts, lineages, and useless laws?

Maybe, though, the Old Testament is like that dusty road. We meet Christ there, but we don't recognize Him.

From Genesis to Malachi, God has painted a portrait of Jesus. He's woven Christ into the ancient traditions and tucked Him inside the laws. Yes, Jesus is in the Old Testament. In many cases, the Hebrew prophets subtly mention Him—there are more than a hundred messianic prophecies sprinkled throughout the Old Testament.[7] In other instances, God commands the Jewish people to actually participate in the foreshadowing of their Messiah— such as in the Feast of Passover.

For thousands of years the Jews lived the promise of Jesus. By using the ordinary backdrop of Jewish life — sheep, bread, and grain — God traced the image of His Son so that when people came face to face with Him, they would recognize Him.

The Old Testament was like Jesus' identification card. After He came to earth, all He had to do was flash it, and those who had been paying attention could identify Him immediately.

Yet many weren't paying attention. Lost in their human traditions, the people of that time did not truly know the Scriptures. Hearing God's Word was more like a religious ritual than an intellectual study. Because people had such little knowledge, they missed the Messiah. They knew they were waiting for a king. They just didn't know He would first suffer to be the King of their hearts.[8]

"You diligently study the Scriptures," Jesus once said, "because you think that by them you possess eternal life. These are the Scriptures that testify about me, yet you refuse to come to me to have life."[9]

Jesus also used the Old Testament to show that He was the predicted Christ. "The Spirit of the Lord is on me," He said, quoting Isaiah 61:1-2, "because he has anointed me to preach good news to the poor. He has sent me to proclaim freedom for the prisoners and recovery of sight for the blind, to release the oppressed, to proclaim the year of the Lord's favor."[10]

The people, though, didn't understand what He was trying to explain.

"Today," He finally said, "this scripture is fulfilled in your hearing."[11]

In other words, "Yes, it's me."

Jesus turned to the ancient Scriptures to prove He was the Messiah.

We should learn from the Master.

The early Christians certainly did. "As his custom was," the Bible says, "Paul went into the synagogue, and on three Sabbath days he reasoned with them from the Scriptures, explaining and proving that the Christ had to suffer and rise from the dead."[12]

Paul, the great missionary and evangelist, used fulfilled prophecies again and again to convince Jews and even Gentiles that Jesus was the Christ.

The people of Berea "examined the Scriptures every day to see what Paul said was true."[13] What did they see? Surely, the same thing we see today—layer upon layer of prophecies.

The Old Testament is like a landscape of rolling hills. From a certain perspective, the hills line up behind each other, looking to be one mountain proclaiming one message. But standing at another viewpoint, it's obvious that there are actually several distinct hills, each declaring different messages. In one paragraph a prophet can warn his people of impending destruction, describe Jesus' first visit to earth, and still give details about Christ's second coming. All these prophecies bump into each other, roll over each other, and sometimes appear as one. With a closer look, though, it's obvious that in the same breath, the prophet spoke of three different times, three different places, and three different experiences.

Sometimes just one verse will carry several distinct meanings. These verses are like the painting that depicts a beautiful young lady, yet at the same time portrays an extremely old woman. That single picture holds two very different portraits. The Scriptures are the same. The longer you look at them, the more you see.

And so this one text, the Old Testament, is many things. Layer upon layer, we discover it as a history book, a praise manual, a guide written from the lives of those who walked before us, a book we won't truly understand until we are no longer reading the words but hearing them in heaven.

Yet the Old Testament is also a picture of Christ—a picture that wasn't given to theologians or pastors or seminary students, but a picture given to everyone, including you and me. God presented Christ in a simple way that we all can understand.

Seeing Jesus in the Old Testament gives us a stronger, more solid understanding of Christ in the New Testament. We develop a clearer view of the way God works, and we equip ourselves with foundational ways to share the salvation message with those searching for the truth.

By using Jesus' example, *Light Before the Son* attempts to uncover His existence within the Old Testament. Each chapter is written in story form. Most of the characters are fictional, but what they learn are scriptural truths. Their imaginary lives serve to teach us the reality of the Bible. From them, we see the Light before the Son.

I hope their stories help you recognize Jesus on your own journey down the road—and in that encounter, to know Him better.

"Do not think that I
have come to abolish the
Law or the Prophets;
I have not come to
abolish them but
to *fulfill them.*"

MATTHEW 5:17

A SECOND LOOK AT
On the Road

And beginning with Moses and all the Prophets, . . .

> The people of Jerusalem and their rulers did not rec-
> ognize Jesus, yet in condemning him they fulfilled the
> words of the prophets.
>
> ACTS 13:27

. . . he explained to them what was said in all the Scriptures
concerning himself. (Luke 24:27)

> He said to them, "This is what I told you while I was
> still with you: Everything must be fulfilled that is
> written about me in the Law of Moses, the Prophets
> and the Psalms."
>
> LUKE 24:44

> Now to him who is able to establish you by my
> gospel and the proclamation of Jesus Christ, accord-
> ing to the revelation of the mystery hidden for long
> ages past, but now revealed and made known
> through the prophetic writings . . . that all nations
> might believe and obey him—to the only wise God
> be glory forever through Jesus Christ! Amen.
>
> ROMANS 16:25-27

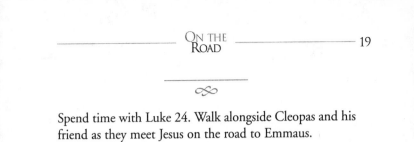

Spend time with Luke 24. Walk alongside Cleopas and his friend as they meet Jesus on the road to Emmaus.

CHAPTER ONE

THE LAMB

Jesus in the Feast of Passover

Jeshua spun around at the sound of his mother's voice. "Don't break the bones," he heard her call.

"Mother?" he whispered as strangers pushed past him.

Certainly it wasn't her. It couldn't have been. She had died several years before.

It was just the wind, he thought. *Besides, even if she were alive, she wouldn't be here, walking toward these bloody crosses.*

Slowly, he turned back toward Golgotha.

If only there were a better way out of town. But there wasn't. That's why all prisoners were crucified there—to make a statement for all travelers to see: obey Roman law or else.

Still, if he could, he'd avoid the Place of the Skull. Two large hollow eyes, a nose, and somewhat of a mouth were worn into the rock. Just one look at the dry, withered hill made his stomach turn. Nature, it seemed, was prepared for what was to come. It knew that death would one day reign there.

A strap on one of his sandals began to bounce with each step. "I should have repaired that last week," he mumbled.

But he was thankful for it now. It kept him from looking ahead—at the skull's watchful eyes.

Quickly, Jeshua pushed through the clamoring crowd. Why would so many people want to see men die? After all, it was Passover. Shouldn't they be with family and friends? So what if Jesus was on the cross? Wasn't it enough to know that he would finally be dead?

And what about his followers? Doesn't it make them sick to see this?

He shook his head as he reached the edge of the crowd and turned toward the busy street.

So many Jews loved Jesus. So many hated him. Frankly, Jeshua felt neither emotion. How could he believe that Jesus was the Messiah when he was dying like a criminal? He doubted there even was a real savior. *We've been waiting and waiting. For what? For nothing.*

"Move it," someone shouted in front of him.

Jeshua looked up to see three soldiers barreling toward him. People scurried to the side of the road. He tried to move but the people blocked his way.

"I said move it!" a soldier again shouted, shoving Jeshua's shoulder.

He stumbled as the soldier pulled out a club.

"Can't you hear?" the guard yelled.

Jeshua nodded, scrambling backward. Quickly, he turned and tripped toward the crowd and the crosses.

"Make way, make way," the soldier commanded.

The mob parted as Jeshua raced through it. He could feel the guard catching his heels. There was nowhere for him to stop. The crowd was too thick. Finally, he pushed to the front and fell at the base of the crosses.

"Oh no," he said, looking up.

He cringed at the gnarly black trees. Nails fastened the men's hands to the branches while the trunks supported their bodies.

"I didn't want to end up here," Jeshua whispered, struggling to his feet.

One of the dying men raised his head and stared at him.

Couldn't the crosses be taller? Why do the men have to die so close to the crowd?

"Let's help the prisoners die," one of the guards yelled, swinging his club toward a cross.

It slammed into the criminal's knees. Jeshua winced as the man jerked and then slumped forward. The nail holes in his hands tore with the weight of his body pulling him down. No man on a cross could survive once his legs were broken. He couldn't push himself up for any last gasps of air.[1]

The Romans considered it merciful.

There's no mercy in killing someone, Jeshua thought.

But the criminals had to die quickly. Obviously, the Jewish Council had requested that the bodies be taken down before morning. After all, during such a holy festival, no Jew wanted to be reminded of death.[2] Or of Jesus.

Jeshua held his breath as the guard approached the middle cross and raised his wooden weapon toward Jesus. But Jesus didn't flinch. The soldier stepped closer. There was no reaction.

"This one's dead," the guard yelled as he dropped his club, letting it hang limply at his side.

"Don't break the bones," Jeshua again heard his mother call.

He turned around. *Why do I keep hearing her voice?* He knew he missed her. But this was going too far.

"Now, Jeshua," he could hear her say, "you must listen to my instructions for preparing the Passover lamb. As you're stretching the lamb out on the cross to cook, be careful with the bones. God has told us not to break any of its bones when preparing or eating it."[3]

How often had he heard those words?

"I know, Mother." That's what he always said. Sure, he didn't understand many of the Feast's details. But he knew how to stretch out the lamb. And he knew that its blood had saved them from Egypt's bondage.

That's why they celebrated the Feast. It reminded them how God killed every firstborn Egyptian son. But for the Israelites, He sent a provision. He told them to sacrifice a lamb and use a hyssop branch to paint its blood on the top and sides of their doorframes.

"When the angel of death saw it, he would 'pass over' the house." Jeshua knew the story by heart.

The blood was a protection, saving those inside. Because of Passover, the Israelites were finally set free from slavery.

But why can't we break the bones? he thought.

No one could ever give him an answer—not even his mother. "There doesn't seem to be a reason," she would say. That was her explanation for all the details of the Feast.

She didn't even know why they had to roast the lamb on a spit.

Why did its inner parts all have to be cooked? Wasn't it easier just to boil it?[4] And why did they have to get rid of the meat before morning?[5]

It's so confusing, he thought, watching the soldiers as they pulled one of the criminals off the cross. Jeshua looked around at the dispersing crowd and then at Jesus. "I guess it's over."

"Remember, the lamb has to be perfect," he again heard his mother say.

"Who said that?" Only a few people still remained. Surely, they didn't know what his mother said every Passover. She had always reminded him and his father of this as they went to pick out the lamb.

But we didn't need a reminder.

Everyone knew the lamb had to be perfect. It had to be a year-old male without defect — those were God's orders.[6] He should know. As a boy, he had to take care of the lamb for five days — God commanded it. Every family picked out their lamb on the tenth day of the month. Then on the fourteenth, they slaughtered it.[7]

"Whatever you do," his father used to say, "keep your sisters away from it."

Sarah and Mary loved all living things.

"We'll take him for a walk," Mary would offer, trying to pry the lamb from Jeshua's arms.

If he ever gave in, he regretted it when the day of the sacrifice arrived. His sisters were always in despair about the lamb's slaughter.

"The lamb is a gift from God," his father would explain. "Only the lamb's blood is able to save us from the angel of death." But the girls still sobbed.

"The lamb wants to die for us because he loves us," his father would go on.

With that, the girls usually stopped crying.

"Well, we love him, too," Sarah would say.

"If you love the lamb, you have to accept him dying for you."

Although Jeshua never admitted it, he could relate to his sisters. After all, he had shed a few tears when no one was looking.

It's just so hard taking care of the lamb, he thought, *and then killing it with my own hands. I mean, the lamb didn't do anything to deserve that—except, of course, be perfect.*

Jeshua looked up again at the soldiers. They pulled the other criminal from his cross.

He glanced back at Jesus.

"A righteous man may have many troubles," he said to himself. It was a psalm he read every Passover. He figured it described the lamb. "But the Lord delivers him from them all. He protects all his bones. Not one of them will be broken. The Lord redeems his servants. No one will be condemned who takes refuge in him."[8]

No one will be condemned, Jeshua thought.

After all, the lamb made sure of it. The Israelites had taken refuge under its blood.

Jeshua stared at the red liquid smeared over Jesus' forehead and hands. He glanced down to a puddle next to a hyssop branch and a sponge covered with vinegar.

Out of instinct, he leaned forward and grabbed the hyssop branch. Just the night before, during the Passover meal, he had used one like it to paint the lamb's blood on his doorframe. Now in the air, oblivious to the soldiers around him, he traced the familiar pattern. He lifted the branch to Jesus' forehead, then in front of his left hand, and finally his right one.

"The cross," he whispered, catching his breath. "Is this what I've been doing all these years? On Passover, have I been sketching a bloody cross—this bloody cross—on my doorframe?"

He dropped the branch and noticed Jesus' legs.

"His bones," he said. "They didn't break His bones."

He felt his heart pound as he saw Jesus stretched out on the cross—like all the Passover lambs.

"Look," he softly called, "the Lamb of God, who takes away the sin of the world."[9] That's what John the Baptist said about Jesus.

But who really believed him? Who believed that Jesus was the saving Lamb of God?

"Let's take the last one down," a soldier ordered. The guards pushed Jeshua back and circled around the cross.

"The lamb must not be left till morning," he heard his mother call.

He shivered as the soldiers tugged on the nails. "He must not be left till morning," he mumbled as he gazed at Jesus' bloody face. It looked so different from when He first rode into Jerusalem—when people hugged Him and talked to Him and walked with Him.

The Pharisees, though, had tried to trap Him with their questions. *But Jesus always answered perfectly,* Jeshua thought.

Just that morning, Pilate himself had said there was no fault in Him.

He's without defect.

"Get out of the way," a soldier shouted. He shoved Jeshua to the ground and stepped over him.

"No!" Jeshua shouted as the soldier drove a spear into Jesus' side.

Blood mixed with water poured out of it.[10] Jeshua quickly reached up and felt the liquid run over his hands, covering the dirt from the road that thickly encrusted them.

At that moment he felt the blood covering much more than just his dusty hands.

The Lamb of God who takes away the sin of the world. Even mine.

When the hour came,
Jesus and his apostles
reclined at the table.
And he said to them, "I
have eagerly desired to
eat this *Passover* with
you before I suffer. For
I tell you, I will not eat
it again until it *finds
fulfillment* in the
kingdom of God."

LUKE 22:14-16

A Second Look at
The Lamb

Prophecy

The LORD said to Moses and Aaron in Egypt, "This month is to be for you the first month, the first month of your year. Tell the whole community of Israel that on the tenth day of this month each man is to take a lamb for his family, one for each household . . . The animals you choose must be year-old males without defect." (Exodus 12:1-3,5)

> *Fulfillment*
> *For you know that it was not with perishable things such as silver or gold that you were redeemed . . . but with the precious blood of Christ, a lamb without blemish or defect.*
> *(1 Peter 1:18-19)*

Prophecy

Take a bunch of hyssop, dip it into the blood in the basin and put some of the blood on the top and on both sides of the doorframe. (Exodus 12:22)

> *Fulfillment*
> *For God was pleased to have all his fullness dwell in [Jesus] . . . by making peace through his blood, shed on the cross.*
> *(Colossians 1:19-20)*

PROPHECY

"The blood will be a sign for you on the houses where you are; and when I see the blood, I will pass over you. No destructive plague will touch you when I strike Egypt." (Exodus 12:13)

Fulfillment
In him we have redemption through his blood, the forgiveness of sins. (Ephesians 1:7)

PROPHECY

"Do not eat the meat raw or cooked in water, but roast it over the fire—head, legs and inner parts." (Exodus 12:9)

Fulfillment
Carrying his own cross, he went out to the place of the Skull. . . . Here they crucified him. (John 19:17-18)

PROPHECY

"Do not leave any of it till morning; if some is left till morning, you must burn it." (Exodus 12:10)

Fulfillment
Because the Jews did not want the bodies left on the crosses during the Sabbath, they asked Pilate to have . . . the bodies taken down. (John 19:31)

PROPHECY

"Do not break any of the bones." (Exodus 12:46)

Fulfillment
The soldiers therefore came and broke the legs of
the first man who had been crucified with Jesus,
and then those of the other. But when they came
to Jesus and found that he was already dead,
they did not break his legs. (John 19:32-33)

These things happened so that the scripture
would be fulfilled: "Not one of his bones will be
broken." (John 19:36)

∞

Look, the Lamb of God, . . .

For Christ, our Passover lamb, has been sacrificed.

1 CORINTHIANS 5:7

Then I saw a Lamb, looking as if it had been slain,
standing in the center of the throne . . . He came
and took the scroll from the right hand of him who
sat on the throne. And when he had taken it, the four
living creatures and the twenty-four elders fell down
before the Lamb . . . And they sang a new song: "You
are worthy to take the scroll and to open its seals,
because you were slain, and with your blood you
purchased men for God from every tribe and language and people and nation."

REVELATION 5:6-9

. . . who takes away the sin of the world! (John 1:29)

Once you were alienated from God and were enemies in your minds because of your evil behavior.
But now he has reconciled you by Christ's physical
body through death to present you holy in his sight,
without blemish and free of accusation.

COLOSSIANS 1:21-22

To him who loves us and has freed us from our sins
by his blood, . . . to him be glory and power for ever
and ever! Amen!

REVELATION 1:5-6

∞

Read the entire Passover story in Exodus 12 along with the
story of Christ's crucifixion in John 19.

CHAPTER TWO

THE BURIED BREAD AND RISEN FRUIT

*Jesus in the Feasts of
Unleavened Bread and Firstfruits*

T he rough rock dug into Abigail's hand, but she could only feel the cold, thick air the cave seemed to be breathing.

It's like a hungry mouth, she thought as she shivered at the four empty pits that bordered the back wall. Why were the graves so skinny and shallow? They were barely big enough to hold a dead, wrapped body.

"Abi," her husband, Adin, called. She pushed away from the chamber, cringing as her shadow skipped over the hollow graves. "You shouldn't be looking at that tomb."

But how could she resist? At least the graves gave her some answers—although she didn't like what they told her.

She glanced at the top of her husband's head bouncing toward her, and then back to the cave.

"How can death look so beautiful?" she whispered, staring at the purple flowers that crept up its jagged entrance. Just like life, the garden had a way of hiding what was on the other side—deep, desperate death.

"You know what those tombs do to you." Adin now stood beside her and pressed his dusty hand against her slender arm.

She nodded, grabbing his powdery fingers.

"Did you cut rock this morning?" she asked.

"Of course not," he said.

She knew better than to ask the question. No Jew did regular work during the Feast of Unleavened Bread.

"I've just been inspecting the tombs."

"You mean the caves," Abigail reminded.

"Yes, the caves."

She wished Adin still hewed cisterns and water tunnels like he did a few years ago. But he enjoyed carving tombs. She wondered how he could spend so much time in those eternal prisons.

"Here's your lunch." She pulled the linen bag from her shoulder and took out a flat loaf of bread.

"Thanks, love." Adin grabbed the roll and broke off a chunk. "Sorry I forgot it."

The bread's heavy scent covered the garden's sweet smell.

"I made it just the way you like—except, of course, without the yeast."

Adin swallowed. "It's still delicious."

But Abigail hated her bread without yeast. It ruined the recipe.

"Besides," Adin said, "we only have to eat it for seven days."

"Right." Abigail sat down on a wide stone bench. "Until next year."

She was tired of celebrating the Feast of Unleavened Bread. She knew it was a command from God, and it had been for hundreds of years, ever since the Israelites escaped from Egypt.

But why do I have to keep eating the heavy bread? she thought. Wasn't it just for the Israelites during the days after their deliverance, teaching them that they'd left the bondage—the yeast—of their old lives behind? Did she have to be reminded of their lesson?

"This is a happy time of year," Adin said, sitting next to her. "We enjoyed last night's Passover Feast, didn't we?"

Abigail shrugged. Passover was nice, but then she had to endure seven more days of the hard bread. After a while, the two festivals just blurred into one.

Adin snapped off another piece and fiddled with its edges.

"Abi," he said softly, "those caves always put you in a bad mood."

She glanced up at the empty black chamber. Its damp air still drifted over to her.

"Last year," she whispered, "that tomb was sealed shut." She squinted at the pits inside of it. "I can't remember what Jesus looked like. But when I see that tomb, I see his body. It's just lying there, lifeless and limp."

"That's what you shouldn't think about," Adin interrupted.

She couldn't help it. Sure, wherever it was, Jesus' body was no longer there. But at one time, it was inside that chamber—dead and rotting.

Abigail took a deep breath.

"I keep wondering if Joseph will reuse the tomb," she said. "I mean, a dead man was inside of it."

"It doesn't matter. By the time Joseph is there, he won't know the difference."

"I suppose so. But really, what kind of man would give away his grave?" Abigail brushed the white powder from Adin's hand and then stood.

"Well, I'd better go. I still have to finish cleaning the house."

"Can't Bani help you?"

"He's not home." Abigail walked backward and then turned around.

"I hope he's not in that dump," Adin called. "I don't know why he likes going there."

❧

A moldy lemon rind rested against Bani's left shoulder, along with a half-eaten melon. He grappled for the ground, feeling slime seep through his fingers, and then dropped his head back onto the rubble.

"Can you help me?" he whispered, looking into the eyes of the man next to him.

But the request was absurd. A dead man could never save him from the pit.

"If I could just push myself like this," Bani grunted, sinking his fingers into the slime. "I know I could make it."

He looked up to the valley's ridge as salty sweat rolled over his lips and into his mouth. His arms quivered and then collapsed. Once again, he slumped into the mire.

"Ever try to get out of here?" he asked the dead man as he wiggled his toes. He couldn't feel pain. He couldn't feel anything, for that matter. "Probably not," he said. "I'm sure you were dead when you got here."

Bani had been staring down at his "companion" when he fell in. That's why he came to the valley. The orange flames that twirled from the garbage were thrilling. But the dead prisoners were much more intriguing.

Bani took a deep breath, tasting the sour air. From the edge of the valley, it never smelled so rancid. Even in Jerusalem, a slight scent always drifted over the city. *But never like this,* he thought.

He glanced at a rotting animal carcass. The Jews didn't sacrifice their children in this valley like the Cannanites once did. Still, the decayed animals and executed prisoners smelled revolting.[1]

"So," Bani grumbled, trying again to push himself up toward the ridge. "How'd you get to the Valley of Hinnom?" He paused and let his arms fold under him. "Oh, maybe you speak Greek," he said. "Then you call it Hell, don't you?"[2]

Bani could hardly remember how he ended up at the bottom of the pit. Tripping over a small bush was the last thing he could recall. The rest of his descent, before he heard his legs break, was a blur.

He closed his heavy eyes and then opened them. *I have*

to stay awake, he thought. *I have to.*

"Have you eaten yet?" he questioned the dead man.

Slime smacked in his ears as he nudged himself toward a piece of flat bread teetering on a broken pot.

"The bread will save me," he said, reaching for its moldy edge, "if I could just get to it."

Certainly it would give him strength.

"If anyone eats this bread," he said, grabbing the air as he fell back, "he will live forever."[3]

Forever? He looked up at the circling vultures. *Did Jesus really mean forever?*

Yes, Bani was certain of it. He had heard Jesus say it himself. Sure, there were a lot of people around. Everyone in Capernaum, it seemed, was gathered there. But Bani understood what Jesus said.

He had been studying under the region's most promi-nent rabbi. Yet when he saw Jesus feed thousands of people with only five loaves of bread, he skipped his classes. Who could study right before the Feast of Unleavened Bread, anyway? He was too excited for his vacation. Besides, seeing a miracle was more interesting that anything he could learn.

"I'm the Living Bread that came down from heaven," he whispered the words of Jesus. "If anyone eats this bread, he'll live forever."[4]

Who could forget those words? It had been two years since he'd heard them, and he still couldn't.

Bani believed Jesus was comparing himself not only to the bread that sustains people, but also to the unleavened bread of the feast. Everyone knew that yeast represented sin. That's why it was never allowed in the temple.[5]

Was Jesus saying that he was the Unleavened Bread? Bani

wondered. *Was he saying he was sinless?*

It's what some people believed. They said that Jesus was perfect and he was able to take on the world's sins. When he died, he suffered the separation from God that everyone deserved. Now, people could live forever.

"Forever," Bani said, looking at the bread. His body shook as he lunged forward. With all of his strength, he grabbed it.

∾

Abigail flicked a small clump of dirt into a clay pot. "This floor won't ever look clean," she mumbled as she squinted down at the small crevices. "Just one crumb of yeast; that's all it takes to ruin the whole feast."

"Abi, are you there?" her friend Narah called from outside.

"Yes," Abigail shouted. She jerked to her feet and hurried to the stone oven. "Your bread is almost ready."

The hot rock stung her skin as she poked the thin dough.

"Just about right," she said, turning and licking the salt from her finger. "It'll be just a little longer. I hope you have time," she called as Narah stepped through the door.

"I have plenty of time," Narah said. "That's because *you're* baking my bread." Her eyes smiled as much as her red lips.

"Good, sit down."

It was always nice to see Narah. It wouldn't be the same if she didn't come every week to buy her bread. Abigail usually tried to talk her into baking her own, but she didn't really want that to happen.

"It's flat bread this week," Abigail said, scrunching her face as she sat down.

"Oh, I love your flat bread."

"You're as crazy as Adin. He just said the same thing to me at the garden."

"Really?" Narah said, "I didn't think you ever went there." Abigail nodded. Narah knew about her distaste for death.

"I had to," Abigail said. "Adin forgot his lunch."

A charred smell stung her nose. She stood and walked over to the oven.

"I looked into one of the caves." She bent over the hot stone and pulled out the bread. "It was Jesus' tomb. Well, you know, the one Joseph gave to Jesus."

"Abi," Narah said quietly, "all of us can give our graves to Jesus."

Abigail dropped the loaves onto the table. She knew Narah and her husband had accepted Jesus as the Christ a few months before. But Narah had never said much about it. And Abigail never asked.

"What are you talking about?" Abigail could feel her heart begin to race.

"You simply can give your grave to Jesus. If you accept that He experienced death for you, you'll never have to die."

Narah walked up behind her. They both folded the hot loaves into white cloths.

"I believe the Feast of Unleavened Bread points to Jesus," Narah said. "He died to clean you of your wrongs." Narah paused and looked around the room. "Just as you've cleaned this house of yeast, Jesus will clean you of your sins. You'll live forever."

That's what Abigail wanted. She didn't want to die in darkness, left for eternity in a small pit within a damp cave.

"You know how the number seven represents completion—like how God made the world in seven days?" Narah said. "Well, the feast lasts for seven days to show that Jesus finished the work of cleaning our sins. It's done. It's over."

Abigail looked down at her dirty hands. How tired she was of cleaning the yeast from her house. How tired she was of fearing death.

"If you want to live forever," Narah said, "all you have to do is give your sin to Jesus—believe that He can clean you."

The front door swung open.

"Smells like bread," Adin called.

Abigail turned quickly toward him. "Oh, I thought you were Bani," she said, trying to keep her voice from shaking. "He's still not home. I was expecting him a while ago."

"I'm sure he'll be back soon," Adin said. "Don't worry, Abi."

She didn't answer.

"Well," Adin said, sitting next to the fire, "I decided to go by our plot of land to see how the firstfruit was growing. It's still tied in a bundle, ready to be harvested."

That's right, Abigail thought, *the Feast of Firstfruits.* She had all but forgotten about it. Who could blame her? It always got lost within the other festivals. After all, it was celebrated in the middle of the Feast of Unleavened Bread—only two days after the feast started.

"Some folks are talking about Jesus and the Feast of Firstfruits," Adin said, looking over at Narah. He leaned against the wall and clasped his hands behind his head.

"Do you know anything about that?"

Abigail didn't breathe, waiting for the answer.

"Well," Narah said, "just as Jesus was buried on the Day of Unleavened Bread, He rose again on the Day of Firstfruits."

Narah gently cleared her throat.

"During the Feast of Firstfruits, the priest waves the first part of each crop before the Lord. The offering represents the rest that will follow." Narah paused. "Jesus is our Firstfruit. He rose from the grave as our representative. Because He was acceptable to God, all of us have become acceptable. We're the harvest that can now follow Him to heaven."

Abigail felt her heart again race as Narah walked toward the door.

"None of us can pull ourselves from the grave," Narah said. "But Jesus did, and He'll do the same for you."

❧

The night air hung like a tent, trapping the stench within the valley. Bani took short, quick breaths. It helped keep the putrid smell from filling his lungs.

"Did you hear that?" he said. "They're searching for me." In between the howls of wild dogs, he listened to the faint muffle of what sounded like his father calling his name.

"Here I am," Bani answered, looking up to the ridge. Yet his voice was but a whisper.

No one will ever find me. I'm going to die here. He glanced at the tall flames burning across the valley. *I'm going to die in Hell.*

He squeezed the flat bread. Blood pumped through his veins.

"No, I won't." He thrust himself onto his stomach.

Scum lodged under his fingernails. He clawed the soggy ground with his right hand and clung to the piece of flat bread with his other.

"My Living Bread," he muttered. "It will keep me alive."

He pulled himself up past the dead man and between two gray trees.

"I give You my yeast, Jesus. Take my sins," he said, amidst the garbage heaps. A spasm ripped through his back and down his legs. His arms caved in, and his chest dropped to the ground. "I believe You saw the pit of death for me—the ultimate separation from God."

He pushed his chest up again.

"Please save me, Jesus."

His whole body trembled as he slowly struggled toward the ledge. Finally dragging himself onto level ground, his arms collapsed once more, his face pressed into the ground. But still, he held onto the bread as if it were life itself.

ॐ

Abigail listened to the birds sing outside the window.

They seem happy, she thought as she looked at Adin and then down at Bani.

"Jesus was born in Bethlehem," she said, reaching out and rubbing Bani's head. His eyes were closed. His breathing was heavy.

"Yes, I know," Adin replied.

"Bethlehem means House of Bread,"[6] she whispered.

"To think, all along Jesus was born to be our Unleavened Bread."

Adin nodded. Before he had found Bani, Abigail had told him that she believed Jesus was the Christ, just like Narah had told her.

"Jesus saved Bani," she said, trying to pry the bread from his hand. Its edges broke away, but he still held on to its core. "I prayed that He would."

"So did I," Adin said softly.

Abigail quickly looked at him.

"When I took the firstfruits to be waved before the Lord," he said, "the only thing I could think of was Jesus' empty grave. The stone couldn't have been rolled away from the inside. The only explanation was that Jesus rose from the dead to be the Firstfruit of all of us."

Abigail felt her eyes sting with tears as she reached out and held his hand.

"Is this heaven?" Bani said. His eyes were barely open.

"You're here with us." Abigail leaned close to him. "You're safe."

"I heard your voices," he said, grabbing onto her arm. "Don't fall into the pit. The dead man can't save you."

"We're here, Bani. We're alive," Abigail said, stroking his forehead. She reached over and touched the unleavened bread in his hand.

"The Living Bread has saved us," he whispered. "We're alive. We're finally alive."

On the first day of the
*Feast of Unleavened
Bread* . . . Jesus took
bread, gave thanks and
broke it, and gave it to
his disciples, saying,
"Take it; *this is
my body.*"

MARK 14:12,22

But Christ has indeed
been *raised from the
dead*, the *firstfruits* of
those who have
fallen asleep.

1 CORINTHIANS 15:20

A Second Look at
The Buried Bread and Risen Fruit

Prophecy

Eat unleavened bread during those seven days; nothing with yeast in it is to be seen among you, nor shall any yeast be seen anywhere within your borders. On that day tell your son, "I do this because of what the LORD did for me when I came out of Egypt." This observance will be for you like a sign on your hand and a reminder on your forehead . . . For the LORD brought you out of Egypt with his mighty hand. (Exodus 13:7-9)

Fullfillment

Get rid of the old yeast that you may be a new batch without yeast—as you really are. For Christ . . . has been sacrificed. Therefore let us keep the Festival, not with the old yeast, the yeast of malice and wickedness, but with bread without yeast, the bread of sincerity and truth. (1 Corinthians 5:7-8)

God made him who had no sin to be sin for us, so that in him we might become the righteousness of God. (2 Corinthians 5:21)

Is not the bread that we break a participation in the body of Christ? (1 Corinthians 10:16)

PROPHECY

The LORD said to Moses, "Speak to the Israelites and say to them: 'When you enter the land I am going to give you and you reap its harvest, bring to the priest a sheaf of the first grain you harvest. He is to wave the sheaf before the LORD so it will be accepted on your behalf; the priest is to wave it on the day after the Sabbath." (Leviticus 23:9-11)

Fullfillment
After the Sabbath, at dawn on the first day of the week, Mary Magdalene and the other Mary went to look at the tomb . . . The angel said to the women, "Do not be afraid, for I know that you are looking for Jesus, who was crucified. He is not here; he has risen, just as he said." (Matthew 28:1,5-6)

Grace and peace to you . . . from Jesus Christ, who is the faithful witness, the firstborn from the dead. (Revelation 1:4-5)

If the part of the dough offered as firstfruits is holy, then the whole batch is holy. (Romans 11:16)

∞

"I am the Living One; I was dead, and behold I am alive . . .

For what I received I passed on to you as of first importance: that Christ died for our sins according to the Scriptures, that he was buried, that he was raised on the third day according to the Scriptures.

1 CORINTHIANS 15:3-4

. . . And I hold the keys of death and Hades." (Revelation 1:18)

Jesus said to her, "I am the resurrection and the life. He who believes in me will live, even though he dies."

JOHN 11:25

"I tell you the truth, whoever hears my word and believes him who sent me has eternal life . . . he has crossed over from death to life."

JOHN 5:24

But we see Jesus . . . now crowned with glory and honor because he suffered death, so that by the grace of God he might taste death for everyone.

HEBREWS 2:9

He was delivered over to death for our sins and was raised to life for our justification.

ROMANS 4:25

∞

Gain a deeper understanding of our Buried Bread and Risen Fruit as you read the following accounts:

Exodus 12:15-20,34 — The Feast of Unleavened Bread
Leviticus 23:9-14 — The Feast of Firstfruits
John 6:1-59 — Jesus, the Bread of Life
Matthew 27:57–28:10 — The Burial and Resurrection of Jesus

CHAPTER THREE

THE NEW GRAIN

Jesus in the Feast of Weeks

Rufus walked toward the chariot, feeling the waves splash behind him as if they were inside his head.

"Must have had too much wine last night," he mumbled, stepping up into the carriage. Thirteen years of sailing had given him sturdy legs. But his stomach still couldn't handle both red wine and the sea.

"That sail had better be securely fastened," he said.

"It is, sir." The driver reached up and tugged on the bundled sail.

"Good." Rufus squeezed into the chariot's rutty wood seat and pointed to the water. "See that ship out there?" The driver turned toward the sea. "That's the biggest ship in Rome. In one trip, it can carry more grain than you, your mother, your brother, and all of your friends will eat in a lifetime."

He paused and watched his ship's naked mast soar stoically above the others. When at port, the ship was never affected by the rocking tide.

"I want this chariot to get to Jerusalem in one piece. Drive smart. Do you understand?"

Rufus didn't wait for an answer. He leaned his head back against the chariot's thin wall and closed his eyes.

"And take the fast route," he yelled as the driver shuffled to the front. The sharp turns would make his head pound worse. But it was worth it. *I just want to get to Jerusalem,* he thought. He could feel the slash ripping across the top of his sail like it was in his own flesh.

The chariot jerked and slowly rolled forward. Rufus opened his eyes and looked out at his ship. Neptune, the god of the sea, was perched high on its stern. Jupiter was mounted on the bow.

No Roman in his right mind would meet the sea without them, he thought as the ship disappeared behind a hill.

A salty breeze blew the thinning hair off his forehead. He watched Caesarea's stone buildings rhythmically roll by until the chariot clattered into the swaying fields. The sharp scent of wheat stung his nose. It smelled almost as good as the pungent sea.

"First barley, then wheat," he muttered.

Every year he followed the same routine. He hauled a ship of barley to Cyprus and Crete. Then, fifty days later, he came back to Israel, picked up wheat, and repeated the run.

He got most of his grain from the Jews. They cut barley

during their holy feast called Firstfruits. Then, on Pentecost—otherwise known as the Feast of Weeks—they harvested wheat. Frankly, Rufus didn't care what they did or how they did it—as long as his ship was stuffed with grain.

"Once you get to Jerusalem," he screamed over the rattling of the chariot's wheels, "go to the Fish Gate and then take the western road."

As usual, he'd leave the tattered sail near the shipwright's front door. Rufus only knew him by his first name—Talmon. Talmon had worked on his sail plenty of times and would have no trouble identifying it.

The chariot spun around a tight corner, catching its wheel on a rock.

"Watch it. Watch it!" Rufus shouted, feeling the carriage lean to the left. He held his breath until it once again settled to its center.

Why couldn't Talmon just live in Caesarea like other shipwrights? Sure, he might have hated the seaport, but so did most Jews. With so many Romans in the city, every Jew had to feel uncomfortable. After all, Pilate even lived there. But it was Talmon's job to fix ships. Shouldn't he be where the ships were? *I guess when you're the best, you can live anywhere you want.*

Besides, Talmon wouldn't work for most Gentiles—only those who had a reputation for being somewhat righteous. If a man showed an interest in the Jewish God, Talmon would repair his ship.

Rufus certainly didn't fit in that category. But his friend Cornelius did. And that was close enough for Talmon.

"Don't forget to turn on the western road," Rufus screamed as the chariot dipped down a bumpy hill. It slid around a bend and into Jerusalem's Fish Gate.

Cornelius—or "the Convert" as Rufus liked to called him—had shown him years ago where Talmon lived. Cornelius was a big man in charge of a hundred Roman soldiers. Rufus respected him, even though he had all but turned away from their religion. He actually believed the Jewish Messiah was coming not only for Jews, but also for Gentiles.

"That's what it says in their holy writings," Cornelius would explain before quoting the same Jewish scripture.

"It is too small a thing for you to be my servant," he would read, "to restore the tribes of Jacob and bring back those of Israel I have kept. I will also make you a light for the Gentiles, that you may bring my salvation to the ends of the earth."[1]

A Savior bringing salvation to me? Rufus thought. *Sure, right.*

"It's this house here," Rufus yelled, motioning to a short building with four square windows. "Gentle with that sail," he said as he climbed out.

Usually, the streets were crammed with people.

"Quiet today, isn't it?" Rufus mumbled.

The driver pulled the sail from the chariot.

"It is, sir. You know, it's Pentecost."

Rufus let out a deep chuckle as he grabbed onto the other side of the sail and the two of them lugged it to Talmon's front door.

"Yes, I know. What an odd feast," he said. "Right now, the Jews are probably waving their two loaves of wheat bread and two sacrificed lambs before their God. Strange people!"

The driver nodded and walked back to the chariot.

"The Jews are coming," he yelled.

Rufus swung around. Masses of long-bearded men crowded the street.

"We can take the back roads," Rufus shouted, racing to the carriage. He climbed in and thrust himself into the seat, just as he heard the sound of a piercing wind.

"What's that?" he yelled. "It's almost like a storm on the sea."

But the sea was miles away. Besides, he'd sailed through plenty of storms. *And I've never seen one like this,* he thought as he looked out at the motionless trees.

Rufus grabbed his ears and stumbled from the carriage. "Wait here."

He followed the mob of Jews as it moved toward a lop-sided house far off the road.

"It's burning," he heard someone shout.

Rufus scrunched his eyes at the yellow flames jumping inside the house. A few men banged against the door.

"Get some water," someone screamed just as the wind stopped.

The house's front door slowly opened and a man stepped out.

A fisherman, Rufus thought. He could tell by the man's rough skin and shabby robe.

Voices came from inside, speaking in the languages of places Rufus had sailed.

"They've had too much wine!" a man shouted. Everyone knew that fishermen were uneducated. How could they speak in different tongues?

"These men are not drunk, as you suppose," the fisherman yelled as he climbed onto a rock. "It's only nine in the morning!"[2] His round stomach jiggled as he laughed.

"Men of Israel," he again shouted, "listen to this: Jesus of Nazareth was a man accredited by God to you by miracles, wonders and signs. You, with the help of wicked men, put Him to death by nailing Him to the cross."[3]

Rufus jerked back. He'd been there during Passover, just over seven weeks before, when the government had crucified Jesus.

"But God raised Him from the dead," the fisherman continued, "freeing Him from the agony of death, because it was impossible for death to keep its hold on Him."[4]

Rufus had heard rumors of Jesus coming back from the dead. Surely, this fisherman didn't expect everyone to believe now, on Pentecost, that he was alive and somehow responsible for the wind and fire.

"God has raised this Jesus to life," the man shouted. "Exalted to the right hand of God, He has received from the Father the promised Holy Spirit and has poured out what you now see and hear."[5]

The Holy Spirit? Rufus thought. How could anyone worship a mere spirit?

"What shall we do?" someone yelled.

"Believe in Jesus Christ for the forgiveness of your sins," the fisherman said. "You will receive the gift of the Holy Spirit."[6]

"This is crazy," Rufus said as he turned and hurried back toward the chariot. Still, he couldn't help but be intrigued. "Forgiveness," he mused, quickly hoisting himself into the carriage.

"What happened, sir?" the driver asked, slamming the door behind him.

"You wouldn't believe it if I told you."

❧

By the time the chariot reached Caesarea, the late afternoon sun had turned the fields to gold. Rufus only glanced at them once; he kept his head down for most of the trip. *How could a spirit make people talk in languages they don't know? And how could it make a fisherman so bold?*

As the chariot rolled into the harbor, Rufus stepped out before it had fully stopped. "I won't need you for awhile," he shouted, walking to his ship. "Don't bother waiting for me."

The long cedar boards creaked when he stepped on deck. He knew the exact spots where they groaned. "Anybody here?" he shouted.

The cavity was hollow. When at port, most of his crew stayed in Caesarea. Turning sideways, he nudged himself down the narrow stairway and walked into his cabin.

"So, if I believe Jesus was crucified to take away my sins," he wondered aloud as he sat down on a chair tied to the wall, "I'll be forgiven and a spirit will live inside of me."

He stared up at the flat ceiling. *Me, forgiven?*

"No," he finally said, "it could never work. Who would forgive a rotten sailor?"

As the days passed, Rufus lost track of time. He hated waiting for his sail. Loading the wheat was the only thing that took his mind off it. That, and thinking of the Holy Spirit.

"You could put words in my mouth," he called one day

to the statue of Neptune. "You could change me. Of course you could."

He turned away, shaking his head. *How can a god get inside of people?*

"Can I come aboard?" A low-pitched voice shouted from below.

Rufus grabbed the railing and looked down. Cornelius stood by the hull, leaning against the beaten wood.

"Sure, come up," Rufus yelled. He pushed away from the railing as Cornelius stepped on deck.

"Did you get lost at sea?" Cornelius called as he walked up and hit Rufus's arm.

"I've just been busy." Rufus wasn't about to explain what happened in Jerusalem or his thoughts about it.

"Well, I figured as much," Cornelius said. "You always try to visit."

He took a step closer and lowered his voice.

"Rufus," he said, "you know that I no longer worship the Roman gods."

"Sure." Rufus nodded.

"And that I've become a believer in the Jewish Lord."

"Yes, you're one of those converts. You and hundreds of other Romans."

"Well, I've seen the Jewish God," Cornelius said. "I've talked to Him. He told me to send my men to Joppa for a Jew named Peter. He'll be at my house tomorrow night."[7]

"You talked to the Jewish God?" Rufus said, letting out a fake laugh.

"I'm telling you, He's going to give us a special message through this Jew." Cornelius took a deep breath. "I think you should be there."

Rufus turned and looked out at the water.

"Listen," Cornelius went on. "I've always said that if a man had to choose between you and the sea, he should pick you because you're the stronger of the two. You might be stronger than the sea, Rufus, but you're not stronger than the Jewish God. One day, you're going to have to face Him."

Is there really anything stronger than the sea? Rufus thought as he stared at the blustery ocean. A gust of air snapped the water against his ship. *Yes, the wind.*

He took another deep breath. "I'll be there."

৵

The next evening came more quickly than the others. Rufus walked to Cornelius's house.

"You're late," Cornelius said as he swung open the front door. He grabbed Rufus's arm and pulled him inside. "Everyone's in there," he said, pointing to a packed room.

Rufus nodded.

"Excuse me," he said, trying to get past a group of men. "Out of my way," he finally shouted, just as the room went silent.

A table creaked. Rufus could tell someone was climbing onto it.

"You are well aware that it is against our law for a Jew to associate with a Gentile or visit him," a familiar voice rang out. "But God has shown me that I should not call any man impure or unclean."[8]

Rufus turned and looked up front.

"It's the fisherman from Jerusalem," he said almost aloud.

"I now realize how true it is that God does not show

favoritism," the man continued, pacing on the uneven table, "but accepts men from every nation. You know the message God sent to the people of Israel, telling the good news of peace through Jesus Christ, who is Lord of all."[9]

Rufus looked around the room. His hands began to sweat. Would the wind come again tonight?

He glanced at several men standing near Peter. Skimming their faces, he stopped. Talmon, the shipwright, stood at the end.

Did he now believe in Jesus, too?

"Jesus Christ is Lord of all," Peter proclaimed. "Everyone who believes in Jesus receives forgiveness of sins."[10]

Rufus felt his heart pound. It almost tickled, like a breeze was inside of him. *Jesus is Lord of all?* he thought. *Even me?*

Quickly, he pushed his way back to the door. Surely, if he could get away from the Jews and their God, the tickling inside him would stop.

But it continued. It fluttered as he ran to his ship, pulling and pushing on every part of him.

"Everyone who believes," he could hear it say, "receives forgiveness."

Rufus dropped to a bench on deck and looked up to the sky.

"Are you stronger than the sea?" he yelled. The wind blew, rocking his ship. "Are you stronger than me?" he shouted. He could feel it swirl.

"Well then, if that's true," he paused, "I believe. Please give me Your forgiveness."

The breeze inside him turned into a gust of wind. It blew over the places he didn't even know were hollow, making them feel whole.

"It's the Holy Spirit." He stared at the sea and then leaned down, resting his head on the bench. "What's going on?" he whispered as he closed his eyes.

"The wind is strong today," a voice called from behind him.

Rufus jolted and swung around. Talmon stood on the edge of the deck with the sail next to his feet.

"I saw you there tonight," Talmon said, stepping over the sail and walking toward him. "You've trusted the Messiah, too, haven't you?"

Rufus nodded. But what could he say? He couldn't explain what had happened to him.

"You now have the Holy Spirit," Talmon said as he sat down next to Rufus. "He was sent here to tell us—to convict us—of our wrongs and to point us to Jesus. He lives in us now. And only through Him can Christ truly be in us."

Rufus could still feel the breeze inside his heart.

Talmon cleared his throat. "The wind, you know, is the unseen power of all ships. If a vessel is to be mighty, it must always yield to the wind."

"Yes, of course," Rufus said, his voice cracking.

"And when you believe in Jesus," Talmon went on, "the Holy Spirit is the unseen power of your life. If you are to be a mighty follower, you must always yield to Him."

"But how?" Rufus asked. He'd never yielded to anyone.

"You must pray and learn God's Word," Talmon said. "You must always allow God's Spirit to blow through your life."

Talmon bent down and picked up a kernel of wheat. "This is the new grain," he said. "For hundreds of years, Jews have celebrated Pentecost by baking two loaves of bread with it. One of these loaves represents the Jews," Talmon continued. "The other is you."

Rufus jerked back, looking at Talmon. "Me?"

"Yes, you, the Gentiles, are symbolized by the other loaf. And the two sacrificed lambs show that Christ died for two nations—for all people." Talmon paused. "The bread is baked with yeast," he continued. "It's made with both the new grain and leaven. As followers of Jesus, we now have both the Holy Spirit and a sinful nature inside of us."

Rufus felt the ship rock with a wave. Water sprayed onto his arms.

"Just as water cleans us, so does the Holy Spirit," Talmon said, holding onto the bench. "He'll change us and make us ready for heaven. It's a struggle, though, because of the sin that's still inside us. But the Holy Spirit is our only chance of surviving the sea."

Rufus stood and walked over to the railing. *Has God's Spirit really come to live in me?* he thought. Talmon followed and rested his elbows against the wood post. In his hands, he played with the kernel of wheat.

"When Jesus was about to be crucified and glorified in heaven," Talmon said, "He explained that if a kernel of wheat died, it would produce many seeds."[11]

He reached over and dropped the kernel into Rufus's hand.

"Jesus was saying that after He died and went to the Father, the Holy Spirit would continue to do God's work through all of us. He will blow through you and tell others about Jesus."

Rufus looked out at the water. Why hadn't he understood this before? It seemed so clear.

He glanced over at the bundled sail. "It looks like my ship can finally go to sea."

Talmon nodded. "Let's put it up."

On each side of the mast they stood, Jew and Gentile. Talmon heaved the rope as Rufus pulled. They worked back and forth until finally the sail soared.

"This is a mighty ship you have," Talmon shouted over the flapping of the sail.

Rufus smiled as he stepped away and looked up at it. "It's nothing, without the wind."

When the day of
Pentecost came . . .
all of them were
filled with
the *Holy Spirit*.

ACTS 2:1,4

A Second Look at
The New Grain

Prophecy

From the day after the Sabbath, the day you brought the sheaf of the wave offering, count off seven full weeks. Count off fifty days up to the day after the seventh Sabbath, and then present an offering of new grain to the LORD. From wherever you live, bring two loaves made of two-tenths of an ephah of fine flour, baked with yeast, as a wave offering of firstfruits to the LORD . . . Then sacrifice one male goat for a sin offering and two lambs, each a year old, for a fellowship offering. The priest is to wave the two lambs before the Lord as a wave offering, together with the bread of the firstfruits. (Leviticus 23:15-17,19-20)

> ### Fulfillment
> *After his suffering, [Jesus] showed himself to these men and gave many convincing proofs that he was alive. He appeared to them over a period of forty days and spoke about the kingdom of God . . . he was taken up before their very eyes, and a cloud hid him from their sight. . . . When the day of Pentecost came, they were all together in one place . . . All of them were filled with the Holy Spirit and began to speak in other tongues as the Spirit enabled them. (Acts 1:3,9; 2:1,4)*

*While Peter was still speaking these words, the
Holy Spirit came on all who heard the message.
The circumcised believers who had come with
Peter were astonished that the gift of the Holy
Spirit had been poured out even on the Gentiles.
(Acts 10:44-45)*

PROPHECY

"It is too small a thing for you to be my servant to restore
the tribes of Jacob and bring back those of Israel I have
kept. I will also make you a light for the Gentiles, that
you may bring my salvation to the ends of the earth."
(Isaiah 49:6)

Fulfillment

*I am not ashamed of the gospel, because it is the
power of God for the salvation of everyone who
believes: first for the Jew, then for the Gentile.
(Romans 1:16)*

*Is God the God of Jews only? Is he not the God
of Gentiles too? Yes, of Gentiles too, since there is
only one God, who will justify the circumcised
by faith and the uncircumcised through that
same faith. (Romans 3:29-30)*

∞

"But the Counselor, the Holy Spirit, whom the Father . . .

"And I will ask the Father, and he will give you
another Counselor to be with you forever — the
Spirit of truth. The world cannot accept him,
because it neither sees him nor knows him. But you
know him, for he lives with you and will be in you."

JOHN 14:16-17

. . . will send in my name, will teach you all things."
(John 14:26)

"But you will receive power when the Holy Spirit
comes on you; and you will be my witnesses in
Jerusalem, and in all Judea and Samaria, and to the
ends of the earth."

ACTS 1:8

Therefore, if anyone is in Christ, he is a new creation; the old has gone, the new has come!

2 CORINTHIANS 5:17

So I say, live by the Spirit, and you will not gratify
the desires of the sinful nature. For the sinful nature
desires what is contrary to the Spirit, and the Spirit
what is contrary to the sinful nature. They are in
conflict with each other . . . But the fruit of the
Spirit is love, joy, peace, patience, kindness, good-
ness, faithfulness, gentleness and self-control.

GALATIANS 5:16-17,22-23

I pray that out of his glorious riches he may strength-
en you with power through his Spirit in your inner
being, so that Christ may dwell in your hearts
through faith.

EPHESIANS 3:16-17

⚭

Follow the Holy Spirit as He reveals Himself throughout
the Bible:

    Leviticus 23:15-21 — The Feast of Weeks

    Acts 1:1-9; 2:1-40; 10:1–11:18 — Pentecost and the
        Salvation of the Gentiles

    John 16:5-16 — The Work of the Holy Spirit

    Ephesians 2:11-18 — The Unity of Jews and Gentiles
        in Christ

    Romans 15:7-13 — The Acceptance of the Gentiles

CHAPTER FOUR

THE SEED

*Jesus in the Seed of Eve and in
the Seed of Abraham*

A tiny black hole dotted one side of the apple. Iscah
spun the piece of fruit around, only to see a larger
dimple on the other side.

"I think a worm got this one," she called down to her
mother. "I'll check to see if he's still inside."

She bit off a sweet chunk and sucked the juice as she
chewed.

"Nope," she said, scooting over on the tree limb, "he
was just passing through."

Worms always gave her the best excuse for eating the
new harvest.

"That's the third apple you've eaten today," her mother
yelled. "If you don't stop, I'm coming up there myself."

But Iscah knew that was impossible. Her mother could

barely walk, let alone climb trees.

"Eve," a voice called from over by the tents.

Iscah looked to see her father holding a thick bundle of weeds.

"There's a thistle in front of your foot. Will you pull it for me?"

Her mother nodded as she slowly bent down and grabbed the thorny plant.

"Ouch," she muttered, heaving it from the ground.

"Thank you," he said as he turned and winked at Iscah.

It was no secret she was her father's favorite daughter. All her brothers and sisters were already grown. As the baby of the family, she could do no wrong. But that was mostly because of her father's memory. He usually forgot her bad deeds.

He's getting so old, Iscah thought as he scuffled away. His years of working on the rocky farmland had taken their toll.

"I'll be right back," her mother called.

Iscah watched her shuffle to the stream and dunk her swelling fingers into the water. Then she centered her gaze on the far-off horizon—at the green, thick foliage that covered the entire plateau.

"Eden," she said softly.

How sorry she felt for her parents. It was hard enough to stand on the outskirts of Eden and dream about what it would be like to live inside. Her parents, though, had actually experienced it. They knew that weeds didn't grow in the garden—only giant flowers did.

And they know what God's voice sounds like, she thought. *How silent life must seem without it.*

Iscah squinted up at the tallest tree that towered over all

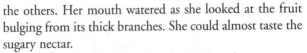
the others. Her mouth watered as she looked at the fruit bulging from its thick branches. She could almost taste the sugary nectar.

There's no use dreaming about it, she thought.

No one could eat from the tree. It was off limits. Just like the rest of the garden, God had banished them from the Tree of Life.[1]

Her parents, after all, had disobeyed God. They ate from another tree called the Tree of Knowledge. But who could blame them? The serpent was so convincing. He said they'd be like God—they'd see good and evil.[2]

"The serpent tricked us. He murdered us."

Now, because of her parents' disobedience, they had to live apart from God.

"I'm going to get another basket," her mother called.

How close her parents seemed to death. Surely, it wouldn't happen too soon, Iscah hoped. But it was so sad they even had to die, especially when they could have lived forever.

She again looked up at the distant garden.

If only we could eat from the Tree of Life, she thought as something slithered under the tree.

"Who's there?" she yelled, looking down at the grass. But she saw nothing.

"I have a secret," she heard a voice whisper, "that will save your soul."

Iscah caught her breath.

"What?" she said, scanning the ground. "Who said that?"

The grass fluttered back and forth, with the movement heading toward the tree.

The serpent, she thought, *of course, it's the serpent.*

"What kind of secret do you have?" she yelled.

No answer. Iscah watched the snake poke its black head up from the grass and then gradually move closer to the tree.

"You can slay me," the voice again hissed. "You can slaughter me and the sin that I sowed. Then, you'll live forever."

Iscah jerked back.

How crazy, she thought. *I must be hearing things*. But then again, maybe not.

After all, it made so much sense. If she could just get rid of the serpent that tricked her parents—if she could just get rid of her sin—then she'd be good enough to get back into Eden. Then she could eat from the Tree of Life.

"All of us could live forever," she said aloud.

She felt her heart pound as the grass quivered underneath her. Quickly, she stood on the trembling branch and jumped feet-first with all her strength, only to realize the serpent had crawled in the grass a few feet ahead.

She raced after the waving wheat.

"I can catch him," she said, crossing the creek. "He's just a skinny snake."

Water soaked into the straps of her sandals and dripped between her toes. Her feet grew heavy with mud and twigs as she gasped for air and climbed the hill. She stopped. Below and behind her, she stared down at her family's tents. They always seemed so small from the plateau.

She looked back again toward the massive garden. *I can't go in there*, she thought, as she felt the snake slither around her legs.

She reached down and grabbed for its scaly body, only to have it slip through her fingers.

"Why can't I kill you?" she yelled, falling to the ground and pounding the weeds.

Out of the corner of her eye, she saw the Tree of Life. "I only want to eat its fruit," she whispered, pushing herself to her feet.

She stared at the angels hovering in front of it. If God's holy guards didn't stop intruders, the sharp sword behind them surely would.[3]

I'll never taste its fruit, she thought.

"Yes, you can," she heard the voice say, "if you make yourself good."

She jolted back as the snake again slinked over her feet.

That's right.

"Iscah, come home," her mother called.

She paused, glancing over her shoulder.

I will, once I've killed him, she thought.

She jumped toward the moving grass, falling onto her stomach.

"I've squashed you!" she screamed, her heart racing.

"Iscah," her mother yelled from behind her. "What are you doing?"

"Umm, nothing really," Iscah said as she rolled over and watched the snake slither away through the grass. She sat up and spun around on her knees.

"I thought I could kill the serpent," she blurted out. "I thought I could kill the sin inside of me. Then I'd be good enough to eat from the Tree of Life."

Her mother sighed, shaking her head. "Oh, Iscah," she said, walking toward her. "You can't make yourself good." She put her hand on Iscah's shoulder. "You can't destroy death or kill the Devil."

"But I want to live forever," Iscah said, scrambling to her feet. "I want all of us to live forever."

"I know," her mother said, grabbing her hand. "So do I, but we have to wait. We have to wait for the Seed."

What was her mother talking about? She'd never heard anything about a seed.

"How can a tiny seed help us?" Iscah said.

Her mother took a deep breath. "I've been waiting until you were old enough to understand."

"Understand what?"

"There's a man who's coming," Eve said. "A Savior who'll destroy your sin and the death it brings."

"A savior? How do you know this?"

"God told us," her mother said. "In the garden, after we disobeyed the Lord, He cursed the serpent. He told him that He would put enmity between the snake and a woman's seed. He said that this Seed would crush the serpent's head, and the serpent would strike the Seed's heel."[4]

Iscah snapped her shoulders back. "The Seed will crush Satan? How can anyone catch him? He's so slinky."

"The Savior will," her mother said, "but first He'll suffer the snake's bite. At one time, I even thought the Seed would come from my body.[5] But I didn't give birth to Him. He'll be born of another woman."

How many years will we have to wait? Iscah thought. *Will people even remember?*

"Does Father know about this?"

"Of course he does. That's why he calls me Eve—the Mother of the Living. He gave me my name after we heard about the Seed. He believes that someday, from our bloodline, the Seed will come. Life will come out of death."[6]

Life, Iscah thought. *We'll finally have life.*

"All you can do," her mother said, "is believe that the Seed will come and conquer death for you."

"But how will we know that He's won?" Iscah stared out at the garden. "How will we know that we can eat from the Tree of Life?"

"I guess the angels will announce it," her mother said.

Iscah looked at the tree. A large piece of fruit dropped off one of its branches, cracking open on the ground. A gust of wind blew a seed from it. For a few moments she watched it whip through the air. Then it whisked up out of Eden, twirling from Iscah's sight.

༄

It blew down through the generations—through the life of Eve's third son named Seth. It blew through Noah and his son and his son after that. It blew through Abraham and Isaac and Jacob and Judah. It whirled through the lives of their descendants—Jesse, David, and Solomon. The Promise blew through Adam and Eve's entire bloodline, generation after generation, until finally, it blew into a cave and into a woman's arms. In Bethlehem, a baby's cry was heard.

༄

When the angels announced that the Son had been born, only shepherds were there to hear their shouts. It happened more than thirty years ago, and nobody really ever thought about it. Few even believed it.

Especially Ithra.

He had too many other things on his mind—like his job.

That's odd, he thought one day as he walked by a Roman soldier standing by a sealed tomb.

The last time he had worked in the garden—only a few days before—the tomb was empty. Its stone was propped up against its chiseled wall.

"Who's in the tomb?" Ithra called, spinning around and walking backward.

"A criminal," the guard grunted, looking straight ahead.

"Well," Ithra said, "I suppose if he's dead, there's no reason to keep watch on him."

The guard slowly looked at Ithra.

"It's my job," he said.

Ithra smiled and turned back around. *How dense can a soldier be?* he thought.

To him, all Romans were intellectually inferior. *They just conquer. They never think things through.*

To some, Ithra didn't seem smart. After all, he was just a simple gardener. "But that's only by choice," he told himself, shaking the seeds in his fist. "I like to work with my hands."

He walked to the far edge of the garden, toward an empty space.

"It's time to grow something here. I can barely look down there anymore."

He stepped near the edge and stared at the place called Golgotha. Three crosses were sprawled over the cracked ground. Black blood had dried where it had dripped over them.

"The Romans still haven't cleaned up their mess," he said.

The execution had occurred a couple days before. Obviously, no one had gotten around to picking up the clutter.

Ithra glanced back at the sealed tomb. *Maybe they buried one of the criminals in there. Maybe it's Jesus.*

But how absurd. Only the rich and righteous were laid to rest in the garden. Convicts weren't given respectable graves.

No, Ithra thought as he bent down and dug a small hole. *They've probably thrown his body in the dump by now.*

He poured several seeds into the crevice and then covered it.

He liked to feel the dirt under his fingernails. It cleared his mind. But it wasn't just the digging he liked. It was all the growing that followed. He was fascinated by it.

How could a broken seed bring forth such life?

"That should do it," he mumbled. Soon, the foliage would be thick enough to block the gruesome sight.

He poured the rest of the seeds into his pouch and began to stroll around the garden. *It almost looks like Eden,* he thought as he brushed his hand over a blooming bush. He wished he could live there—back before Adam and Eve were cast out. How badly he wanted to be that close to God, to live without sin.

Once he heard his rabbi explain that God would someday destroy death. He said a woman's Seed would crush Satan.

"I'll put enmity between you and the woman," Ithra recited the prophecy his rabbi quoted. "And between your seed and her Seed. He will crush your head, and you will strike His heel."[7]

Ithra shrugged, letting a seed tumble into another hole he'd dug. *What's the use of waiting for the so-called Seed?* he thought.

Long ago, he'd decided to take things into his own hands. *I can destroy death and the sin inside of me. It's as simple as following the Law. If I obey, I'll be good enough for God.* He leaned back on his knees and brushed the dirt from his hands. *Then I'll live forever.*

And besides, the Mosaic Law was so enticing. By making himself good, he got all the credit.

Still, even with all of his logic, he couldn't understand one thing. Like most Jews, he considered his forefather Abraham to be an upright man. *After all,* he thought, *God called him righteous.*

But Abraham lived before the Ten Commandments— before the Law was even established. And on top of that, there were some aspects of his life that were undesirable. He resided among pagan worshipers. And when God called him to leave without his family, he brought along his nephew, Lot.[8] He also lied to the Pharaoh of Egypt, telling him that his wife, Sarah, was only his sister.[9]

How could God call him righteous?

Ithra knew the answer. He just tried to avoid it.

God had given Abraham a promise. He said that from Sarah's barren womb, a seed would come. From this Seed, there would be countless descendants—as many as the stars, if they could be counted. Abraham believed, and the Lord credited it to him as righteousness.[10]

"He believed in the Seed," Ithra said to himself. "He believed that life would come out of barrenness—out of death."

Ithra felt his hands sweat.

Abraham wasn't righteous because he was good or because he followed God's laws. He was righteous because he had faith in the coming Seed. The only thing I can do is believe. Believe in the same Seed promised to Adam and Eve.

After all, Abraham was from their bloodline.

"But how can I believe in the Seed?" he said to no one but the vines climbing the stone wall. "I don't know how."

Suddenly the ground beneath Ithra's feet trembled so hard he fell onto his knees.

The sealed tomb nearby quivered as a light shone within it. The stone burst back and slammed against the side of the cave. Perched on top was a man in a pure white robe shouting, "He has risen!"

Ithra jerked back. He watched the Roman soldier scramble toward the cave and poke his head inside.

"The dead has come to life!" the soldier shouted as he ran to the garden's gate.

But how can that be? Ithra could hardly breathe as he stared at the tomb.

One by one, long strips of linen flung into the air and landed at the cave's entrance. Slowly, a man's head appeared and then his face. He ducked under the cave's opening and stepped out into the garden.

"But who could defy the grave?" Ithra whispered. "Who could destroy death?"

He felt his heart pound faster.

"The Seed," he gasped, watching the man disappear into the trees. "Of course, the Seed."

Ithra ducked behind a bush as two women ran in front

of him. A jar of burial spices dropped at their heels and rolled next to Ithra.

"He's gone!" one of the women yelled as they rushed away.

Ithra didn't say a word. How could he even begin to explain what had just happened?

Has the Seed really come? he thought. *Has He just conquered death and crushed the hold that Satan has had on us?*

Ithra could run after the man and ask him. But his body felt frozen.

It wasn't long until the women returned with two men. Ithra watched as they entered the cave.

"He's alive," one of the men shouted as they ran toward the garden's entrance.

"Excuse me," Ithra yelled. "Do you know who was buried there?"

The men kept running.

"Gentlemen," he again yelled, heading after them. "Do you know who was just raised to life?"

One of them stopped.

"It was Jesus," the man said. "I'm sure you've heard of Him."

Of course Ithra had heard of Him. People claimed He was sent by God.

"Jesus told us this would happen," the man continued. "Why didn't we understand? He said He'd be raised to life."

Ithra could barely catch his breath.

"It seems so silly, though," the man said. "Why did He have to die, only to come back to life? What's the use?"

"Are you crazy?" Ithra blurted out. "Don't you see? He's the Seed of Eve. He had to die. That's the only way He could crush the serpent. He had to rise from the dead to conquer death."

Ithra's mind spun. *That means He's also the Seed of Abraham. If I believe in Him—like Abraham did—I'll be counted righteous.*

"People used to believe in the Seed that would come," Ithra told the man. "Now, we can believe in the Seed *who's here.*"[11]

He scanned the garden.

"Jesus is the new Tree of Life. All who come to Him will live forever. And maybe now that He's alive, He'll someday kill Satan once and for all."

The man stepped forward.

"How do you know all this? Who are you?"

"I'm the gardener," Ithra said and then paused. "It's my job to study seeds."

The promises were spoken to Abraham and to *his seed*. The Scripture does not say "and to seeds," meaning many people, but "and to your seed," meaning one person, *who is Christ*.

A SECOND LOOK AT
The Seed

PROPHECY

"And I will put enmity between you and the woman, and between your seed and her Seed; He shall bruise your head, and you shall bruise His heel." (Genesis 3:15, NKJV)

> *Fulfillment*
>
> *An angel of the Lord appeared to [Joseph] in a dream and said, "Joseph son of David, do not be afraid to take Mary home as your wife . . . She will give birth to a son, and you are to give him the name Jesus, because he will save his people from their sins." (Matthew 1:20-21)*
>
> *This grace was given us in Christ Jesus . . . who has destroyed death and has brought life and immortality to light through the gospel. (2 Timothy 1:9-10)*

PROPHECY

Then the word of the LORD came to [Abram] . . . "Look up at the heavens and count the stars—if indeed you can count them." Then he said to him, "So shall your off-spring be." Abram believed the LORD, and he credited it to him as righteousness. (Genesis 15:4-6)

Fulfillment

*Against all hope, Abraham in hope believed and
so became the father of many nations . . . This
is why it was "credited to him as righteousness."
The words "it was credited to him" were written
not for him alone, but also for us, to whom God
will credit righteousness—for us who believe in
him who raised Jesus our Lord from the dead.
(Romans 4:18,22-24)*

───────
∞

"Your father Abraham rejoiced at the thought . . .

Since the children have flesh and blood, he too
shared in their humanity so that by his death he
might destroy him who holds the power of death—
that is, the devil—and free those who all their lives
were held in slavery by their fear of death.

HEBREWS 2:14-15

. . . of seeing my day; he saw it and was glad." (John 8:56)

The reason the Son of God appeared was to destroy
the devil's work. No one who is born of God will
continue to sin, because God's seed remains in him;
he cannot go on sinning, because he has been born
of God.

1 JOHN 3:8-9

Then they asked him, "What must we do to do the works God requires?" Jesus answered, "The work of God is this: to believe in the one he has sent."

JOHN 6:28-29

What, then, was the purpose of the law? It was added because of transgressions until the Seed to whom the promise referred had come ... So the law was put in charge to lead us to Christ that we might be justified by faith.

GALATIANS 3:19,24

∽

Follow the Seed as He travels from Eden to the empty tomb:

Genesis 3 — The Fall and the Promise of the Seed

Genesis 15:1-6 — Abraham's Belief in the Seed

John 20:1-9 — The Empty Tomb

Romans 4:13-25 — Abraham's Faith

Galatians 3:1-28 — The Seed and the Law

CHAPTER FIVE

THE NEW COVENANT

Jesus in the Mosaic Law

T he small stone dangled from its gold chain, swaying on Mahlah's neck to the same rhythm as her footsteps.

"It's so beautiful!" she said softly, reaching up and feeling its jagged bumps. A few drops of blood still looked red against the rock's surface. Most of it, though, had darkened as it dried.

I should clean it, she thought. *But that would make it less special.*

The bloodstain symbolically bound her to God. Surely, that's what Moses had in mind when he sprinkled it over her and the other Israelites.

"This is the blood of the covenant," he shouted after

reading God's commandments, "that the Lord has made with you in accordance with all these words."[1]

The commandments and laws were tough and rigid. Even so, all the Israelites said they could obey them. They believed they were good enough to keep them. The blood sealed their agreement. Now there was no turning back.

"Adah," she beckoned, stopping in front of a dirty tent, "are you there? It's me, Mahlah. I have something to show you."

The tent quivered before its leather door flapped open.

"She's not here." Adah's mother stepped out from the darkness. Mahlah recoiled at the sweaty scent. The wilderness made everyone smell bad. But this woman always had a more wilting odor than most.

"Well, please tell her I was here." Mahlah quickly turned, feeling her necklace swing with her.

"Wait." The woman grabbed her arm, causing her to stumble. "What's this?" She ran her bent finger over the necklace's rough gold.

"Oh, I came to show it to Adah," Mahlah said, stepping away. "My father gave it to me so I'd remember God's laws. He found the stone at the base of Mount Sinai after we heard God's commandments. And I was wearing it when Moses read the laws again. You know, just before he splashed the blood on us."

Mahlah glanced down at the long chain. It was the prettiest of all the jewelry that her father had taken from Egypt.

"It's perfect," the woman said.

"I know, isn't it?"

"Yes, the gold will be perfect for making our new god."

"A new god?" Mahlah clutched the stone. Its ridges dug

into her skin. "But we already have one. You heard Moses
before he went back up the mountain. You heard the commandments. The first one says we can't have another god."

"Oh, fish tails," the woman spit. "The more gods, the
better. Do you want to get out of this desert?"

Mahlah stared at her rough, reddened toes. They burned
from the heat.

"But if we obey the laws," she said, "God will bless us."

"Does this desert look like a blessing?"

Mahlah eyed the rows of ripped tents and then turned
back to Adah's mother.

"Face it," the woman snapped. "Moses is dead and so is
his God."

Mahlah shivered at the thought.

"You know, he's been gone for days," the woman continued. "Him and some of his elders. Isn't *your* father missing, too?" The woman pointed to the charred Mount Sinai.
"Just look up there. How could anyone survive all that
smoke?"

"But my father . . . "

"It doesn't matter about your father now. He can't protect
you. What you need in this desert is someone who can."

Mahlah's hands went numb as she released the stone
pendant. Could the woman be right? What if her father
was hurt? Or even worse, dead? He'd never been gone for
so long. Now how could she believe in a God who would
take her father from her?

"If you'll just give me your necklace," the woman said,
stepping behind her, "you'll have a new god."

Mahlah's heart ached as the woman fumbled with the
gold chain.

"This is the right decision," the woman soothed, pulling it from Mahlah's neck. "Your new god will be here tonight. Oh, and I'm sorry about your father." She ducked inside her tent.

Mahlah grabbed her bare neck. Why did her father have to leave? Her throat throbbed as she turned and walked toward the open field.

At least I'll have a god, she reasoned, sitting on a large rock. She hoped this one wouldn't be so cruel as to take away her father.

Eventually, shouts and cheers echoed from the other side of camp. As the sun began to set, she saw smoke rise against the sky.

"Mahlah," a voice suddenly called from behind her.

Chilled, she twisted around.

"Daddy!" She gasped as she ran and flung her arms around his waist. "I thought you were dead."

Was it really him? *Has he come back?* she thought, pressing her face into his musty robe. It turned wet with her tears.

"I needed time to think, Mahlah," he said as he lifted her chin. "I saw God—we all saw Him."

"God?" she gasped, wiping her drenched cheeks.

"Yes. We ate and drank with Him."[2]

"With God?" Mahlah could hardly believe it. No one but Moses had ever been in His presence.

"We did." Her father wrapped his arm around her shoulder and walked forward. "After we agreed to keep the covenant, He was at peace with us. And it's all because we said we'd follow His laws."

Laws? Mahlah thought as a hot breeze blew over her

neck. She'd forgotten about the laws. *How will I explain the missing stone?*

"What wrong?" her father asked.

Mahlah swallowed hard and then pointed to the thick haze of smoke.

"I gave my necklace away. They're using it to make another god." She looked up at her father. "You weren't here, and Moses wasn't here. I thought God left us. I thought you were gone forever. I didn't know what to do."

"A new god?" Her father dropped his arm from her shoulder and began to run toward the camp. "But Moses is still with the Lord!"

Mahlah lifted her robe and raced after him.

"I'm sorry," she yelled, running past row after row of tents.

When they reached the far side of the camp, her stomach sank as she watched people dancing around a gold calf perched high on a fiery alter. How small and useless it looked. Its crooked legs and skinny body could never protect anyone.

"A calf," her father whispered. "It's a silly golden calf."

Mahlah squinted down at his tears splashing on the dirt.

"Do you know why God gave us His laws?" her father said, his voice cracking. Mahlah's head spun. She couldn't think.

"Three reasons. The laws show us who God is," her father said. "They also show us who we are—the things that are inside of us. The things we shouldn't be."

Mahlah rubbed her neck. "What's the third reason?" she whispered.

"To make us holy," her father said. "But it's failed."

Failed?

"God gave us those laws," Mahlah said. "He should have known we would break them."

"I think He did," her father said. "We're the ones who didn't."

"But, Daddy," Mahlah grabbed his arm, "you haven't broken the commands."

"Oh, I will. Just look at them." He shook his head. "We thought we could keep God's laws, but we're not good enough."

Mahlah watched as he turned and walked away. He never looked back. Why would he? Who would want to look at an idol after seeing the Lord?

"I'll never worship it," Mahlah promised, casting a scornful gaze at the calf.

What a useless thing to say. She'd already broken the covenant.

❧

Later, when Moses returned, the idol was destroyed anyway. He smashed the tablets inscribed with the Ten Commandments and then burned the flimsy calf.

The shattered stone was like their promise to God—broken.

Still, Moses went again to the mountain. Finally, after forty more days, he carried back two new stone tablets, again chiseled with the Ten Commandments.

"These are the laws your Lord has given you," he screamed once more.

With each command, Mahlah's father kicked the dirt.

"We're stuck in this covenant," he said as ashes from the

idol drifted up from the ground. "We made the agreement. Now we have to live with it."

Mahlah stared at his foot. Under his heel, she could see a small rock attached to a gold chain.

"My necklace." She fell to her knees and grabbed it. "Someone must have dropped it."

She could hardly breathe as she pushed it into her father's hands.

"There's a crack in it," he observed.

"Like our covenant," Mahlah said. "But I can still wear it." She turned and lifted her hair, feeling the crushed chain drape around her neck.

"Father," she said, "when we were given God's commands, what if we admitted that we weren't good enough to be holy? Do you think He would have given us another way?"

"I don't know," her father said. "All we can do is hope that He'll offer us a new covenant."

Yes, of course, Mahlah thought, *maybe God will give us a new covenant.*

❧

A jagged link in the gold chain jabbed Chloe's neck as she leaned forward and peeked through the door's tiny knothole.

This silly necklace, she thought, rubbing her tender skin. She hated wearing it, but her father insisted. Ever since she could remember, the stone had dangled around her mother's neck—and before that, her grandmother's. Now, it was her turn to wear it.

Quickly, Chloe scanned the men sitting around the

wide, short table.

"Great place to eat the Passover," the biggest man said, looking up at the black wood that paneled the low ceiling and then over at the peeling walls.

"Probably the best upper room in Jerusalem," the man next to him muttered.

Jesus nodded as He pulled Himself toward the table. "It's time for the wine."

The men fumbled for their clay goblets as Jesus lifted the carafe and poured out a portion.

"This cup," He said slowly, pausing as a few drops of red wine splashed onto the table. "This cup," He again said, "is the new covenant in my blood which is poured out for you."[3]

The new covenant? Chloe jerked back. Her stone pendant flung forward, knocking into the dry wood. She caught it with her hand.

How many times had she heard about the new covenant? Her necklace was a reminder of the first agreement the Israelites had made with God.

"But the new covenant will be better," her father always said.

Chloe brushed her thumb over the necklace's cracked stone and remembered the words of the prophet Jeremiah: "The time is coming," declares the Lord, "when I will make a new covenant with the house of Israel. It will not be like the covenant I made with their forefathers when I took them by the hand to lead them out of Egypt, because they broke my covenant."[4]

"I will put my law in their minds and write it on their hearts," Chloe now repeated the words. "I will be their God, and they will be my people. For I will forgive their wickedness and will remember their sins no more."[5]

She squeezed the stone and leaned forward, watching Jesus stand to His feet.

"The new covenant," she whispered, "is here."

But how would it be in His blood?

The roof shook as the men scrambled behind Jesus to the door.

I should tell someone, Chloe thought, stumbling down the outside stairs. She hid by a crooked window. Surely, her father would want to know. But he would never let her follow them.

Twigs snapped under the men's feet as they walked toward the road.

I'll tell him later.

She ran up a hill and down the other side until the men stopped under a tall gate.

"The Garden of Gethsemane," she said to herself, squinting as Jesus walked into the garden and over to a large rock.

Hurrying after Him, she dropped to the ground and crawled between bushes—as close as she could to where He sat.

"Father," she heard Him say, "if You are willing, take this cup from me."[6]

No, she thought, *He can't give away the cup of the new covenant.*

Jesus pressed His cheek against the flat stone.

"Yet not my will," He said as a light moved toward them, "but Yours be done."[7]

Chloe looked up at what appeared to be a couple dozen burning torches bouncing closer and closer.

Soldiers, she realized, as the outlines of bulky bodies
came into focus. *Why would soldiers be in the garden so late
at night?*

"Who do you want?" Jesus asked.

Chloe cringed as a man walked over and poked a sword
into Jesus' chest. Quickly, the soldier dug a fist into His side.

It wasn't until they dragged Jesus away that she crawled
from the bush and ran for home.

Her father would be outraged at His capture. But she
couldn't tell him. He'd probably chase after Jesus. Surely,
he'd be killed himself.

Besides, she thought as she slowly opened the door,
everyone's asleep. I'll tell him in the morning.

She held her breath as she crept through the dark
rooms. No one, it seemed, had even missed her. During the
Feast, with all the extended family in town, it was easy to
get lost in the crowd.

Chloe fell back onto her mattress and closed her eyes.
Her body still shook from fear.

❧

"They have Jesus!" someone outside shouted. Chloe
abruptly sat up and squinted at the sunlight. "The Romans
have Jesus!"

She jolted off the cushion.

"Let's go," her father yelled as he rushed into the room.

"What's happening?"

"The Romans are going to crucify Jesus!" he yelled. "I
just heard it."

Crucify Him? Chloe felt her heart stop.

"Pilate gave his judgment early this morning—that's what people are saying." Her father grabbed her arm and rushed out the door.

They merged with the crowd into the street. If they could just get to the palace, they could help plead His case.

"He's coming," someone shouted. "They've beaten Him. He's carrying a cross."

Already? Chloe thought. *Of course, the earlier, the better.* That way, the Romans and the Jewish Council could avoid His followers.

Chloe's father reached back and pulled her to the side of the road. A gnarled piece of wood quivered toward them.

"Jesus," she whispered. Blood streamed down His forehead, dripping onto the ground. It covered His back and stained the cross.

"Jesus!" she screamed, reaching out for Him.

His blood splashed onto her hand. She jerked back from the pushing crowd, catching her gold chain on someone's robe. She felt it break and slip from her neck.

"Father," she cried. "My necklace. It's gone."

"Leave it." He pulled her through the crowd. "We need to follow Jesus."

Chloe could barely see as they pushed their way toward Golgotha. She watched the first cross sway into the air, holding its prisoner tight. Finally, when they got closer, she saw Jesus' cross swing into place. Now He was dying, but He'd never explained how they could make a new agreement with God.

Quickly, she turned. She couldn't watch. Her father called out as she ran toward home. But she didn't look back.

"God, why didn't You give us the new covenant?" she yelled into the air. For days, she asked the same question.

But there was no answer—not until she heard people again teaching about Jesus.

"Jesus is the Law that can now be written on your heart," one of His disciples said. "He is the only One who kept the Law. He is the Perfect Law. Now, He'll live inside you and help you follow God's commands."

Jesus, inside of me? Chloe thought.

"If you agree to follow Him, His blood will seal the covenant. God will now be at peace with you."

Chloe needed Jesus to be written on her heart. She couldn't be good on her own.

She looked down at her chest—to where the necklace used to hang.

Finally, I have what I cannot lose.

Christ is the
end of the law
so that there may
be *righteousness*
for everyone
who *believes*.

ROMANS 10:4

Christ is the
end of the law
so that there may
be *righteousness*
for everyone
who *believes*.

ROMANS 10:4

99

A SECOND LOOK AT
The New Covenant

PROPHECY

"The time is coming," declares the LORD, "when I will make a new covenant with the house of Israel and with the house of Judah. It will not be like the covenant I made with their forefathers when I took them by the hand to lead them out of Egypt, because they broke my covenant . . . This is the covenant I will make with the house of Israel after that time," declares the LORD. "I will put my law in their minds and write it on their hearts. I will be their God, and they will be my people . . . For I will forgive their wickedness and will remember their sins no more." (Jeremiah 31:31-34)

Fulfillment

The former regulation is set aside because it was weak and useless (for the law made nothing perfect), and a better hope is introduced, by which we draw near to God. (Hebrews 7:18-19)

Therefore no one will be declared righteous in his sight by observing the law; rather, through the law we become conscious of sin. But now a righteousness from God, apart from law, has been made known, to which the Law and the

*Prophets testify. This righteousness from God
comes through faith in Jesus Christ to all who
believe. (Romans 3:20-22)*

*For if there had been nothing wrong with that
first covenant, no place would have been sought
for another . . . By calling this covenant "new,"
he has made the first one obsolete; and what is
obsolete and aging will soon disappear.
(Hebrews 8:7,13)*

∞

The law is only a shadow of the good things that are coming . . .

So the law was put in charge to lead us to Christ
that we might be justified by faith. Now that faith
has come, we are no longer under the supervision of
the law.

GALATIANS 3:24-25

. . . not the realities themselves. (Hebrews 10:1)

He forgave us all our sins, having canceled the written code, with its regulations, that was against us and
that stood opposed to us; he took it away, nailing it
to the cross.

COLOSSIANS 2:13-14

Therefore, there is now no condemnation for those
who are in Christ Jesus, because through Christ Jesus

the law of the Spirit of life set me free from the law of sin and death. For what the law was powerless to do in that it was weakened by the sinful nature, God did by sending his own Son in the likeness of sinful man to be a sin offering.

ROMANS 8:1-3

The sting of death is sin, and the power of sin is the law. But thanks be to God! He gives us the victory through our Lord Jesus Christ.

1 CORINTHIANS 15:56-57

I do not set aside the grace of God, for if righteousness could be gained through the law, Christ died for nothing!

GALATIANS 2:21

∞

Take a deeper look at God's covenant—no longer written on stone, but on our hearts:

Exodus 19–20, 24, 32, 34—The First Covenant
Luke 22:7-20, 39-44—The New Covenant

CHAPTER SIX

THE
WEARY'S REST

Jesus in Canaan and in the Sabbath

The thin leaves crunched under Eliab's sandals as he stepped closer to the bush and dug his hand between its prickly branches.

"All I want is fruit," he mumbled. "Is that too much to ask?" He grabbed a thorny limb and quickly jerked his hand away.

"Eliab," his wife, Nasha, called. He looked up to see her walking backward, dragging their overstuffed bag. "You'd shake a weed if I let you. Now hurry up, or we'll be left behind."

Eliab glanced at the mob of Israelites moving past him and then back to the bush. *There'll never be fruit in the wilderness,* he thought, giving it one last nudge.

Finally, he shuffled past the people.

"Let's talk about grapes," he said once he'd caught up with her.

He pulled the bag from her hands and held it in his bony arms.

"I'm tired of thinking about food," she muttered. "We've talked about it ever since we left Egypt."

She's right, Eliab thought. Who could argue with her? He couldn't. He hadn't won an argument for decades — ever since they were married.

"Maybe you should start counting cracks again," she said.

Eliab looked down at the crusty desert floor. He'd forgotten how many he'd counted. After all, they'd been in the wilderness for almost forty years.

There's no way to remember all those numbers, he thought, wiping the sweat from his wrinkled face.

If only he could find some shade. There wasn't even a tree in the desert — just cowardly bushes that didn't have enough strength to battle the heat. Often he was tempted to cool off by rolling up his sleeves. But how could he look at all those scars? The whip marks only reminded him of his friends who had died in chains — their bones lost somewhere in the sands of Egypt.

I guess I could be dead, he thought.

Still, life seemed better back then. He could almost taste the leeks and cucumbers. *Now, we just get manna.*

Like everything in the wilderness, the thin wafers that God scattered on the desert floor were decent, but not a delight. Life was meager, not to mention tedious. How

many times could they pass by the same bush? They
walked in circles—always en route, but never reaching the
Promised Land.

They were saved from Egypt's slavery, but stuck in the
weary wilderness.

"The cloud has stopped," Nasha suddenly said.

Eliab looked up at the puffy white ball hovering in front
of them. Whether they liked it or not, the cloud determined their course. God, after all, was in there.

He's not a very good guide, Eliab inwardly accused, trudg-
ing up a sandy hill. *We can't even get to Canaan.*

Yet everyone knew it wasn't God's fault. It was just easier to blame Him. God had led them to the edge of Canaan
and said He had given them the land. The Israelites were
the ones who refused to enter.[1]

Giants were in there, Eliab remembered. *We didn't think
God could fight giants.*

The Lord might have saved them from Egypt's slavery,
but the Israelites didn't believe He could conquer Canaan.

Eliab paused at the top of the hill. "Now, we'll never see
the Promised Land," he said.

God had made sure of it. Eliab's entire generation had
to wander in the wilderness for forty years. That's what
God promised. As soon as every unbelieving man died, the
next generation would be able to enter Canaan.[2]

Eliab's soul ached as he surveyed the valley below.
Masses of Israelites began to cover the land. Not one man
from his generation was among them. They had all died.
Soon, it would be his turn.

We'll be buried, he thought, glancing over at Nasha, *in
that dreary sand.*

"Let's go," Nasha said, grabbing onto his arm. "Jared will be waiting."

Eliab smiled, thinking of his son. *At least he'll be able to live in Canaan,* he thought as he scuffled down the hill.

Jared usually traveled ahead of them. That way, he could get his wife and children settled before helping them with their tent.

"At last, we're here," Nasha said as they walked toward their tribe. "We can finally rest."

Eliab dropped the bag. Both of them slowly bent their knees and sat on it.

Rest? he thought. *I haven't rested for forty years.*

Sure, he kept the Sabbath. It was one of God's Ten Commandments. No one could do regular work on the seventh day. Eliab never even searched for fruit or repaired his tent. He wore his clothes smelly so Nasha didn't have to wash them.

But in my heart, Eliab mused, *I can never rest.*

He worried about nations attacking and toiled over the lack of good food. *I wish God could make my mind rest as well. It's my anxious heart that makes me so tired.*

Yet Moses said that when they entered Canaan, the land would finally give them rest.[3]

It made sense. The towns were already fortified. They stood strong and tall, waiting to protect the Israelites from attacking nations. The fields were plowed and seeded. The grapevines were waiting to pour forth their juice. In Canaan, others had already done the work for them.[4]

It was the ultimate kind of rest. But it would never be his.

"Good, you're safe," he heard his son call. "Just give me a chance to set up your tent and then you can sleep."

Eliab nodded as he watched Jared unfold the dirty cloth. He grabbed Nasha's hands and pulled her up as he stood.

"Maybe tonight will be the night," she said as she teetered to her feet.

"Don't say such a thing." He leaned down and kissed her. "You still have a few years left in you."

But he knew she didn't.

We don't have years, he thought. *We'll be lucky if we have days.*

After Jared finished pitching the tent, Eliab and Nasha crawled inside. Nasha relaxed on her dirty blanket, her heavy breathing becoming shallow.

Eliab stared skyward as the evening breeze flapped away at the tent's torn ceiling. *Even the night doesn't allow me to rest,* he thought.

He slowly closed his eyes and then felt Nasha grab his shoulder.

"I love you," she gasped.

He twisted toward her. Her eyes were closed.

"Nasha," he whispered.

She never opened them.

"O Nasha." He dropped his head to her chest.

❧

During the days that followed, Eliab prepared for his own death. He was the last one, except for Moses, who had to die before the new generation could enter Canaan.

"When you enter the resting place," Moses would say to the new generation, "you're not to live as your fathers did in the desert—everyone as he saw fit."[5]

Eliab didn't need to be reminded how they had lived.

We've had such little faith, he thought as he lay back, trying to catch his breath between sharp pains in his chest.

He looked up at the thin clouds and thought about his days in the wilderness.

"It's been so hard," he said in a near whisper, grabbing his son's hand and pulling him closer. "Remember me." His words faded. "Remember me when you enter the rest."

❧

After Eliab died, not even a stone was set up to mark his grave. The new generation had no time to lose. Canaan was waiting. They understood what their fathers didn't. The desert of disbelief was a waste of time.

God had already given them the Promised Land.

"The Lord has surely given us the whole land," the new generation shouted before they marched into Canaan. "The people are melting in fear because of us."[6]

During all those years in the desert, their fathers had no idea that the Canaanites were actually terrified of their God. So much so that they were planning to almost hand over the land without a fight. If the Israelites would have just stepped in, every valley, hill, and town could have been theirs.[7]

❧

Eliab yawned and rubbed his tired eyes as he sat in the dim room. His eyes, he was told, resembled those of his ances-

tor who long ago had wandered the wilderness. Eliab
wasn't sure; he'd never met the man he was named after.

Why am I even here? he thought, glancing around the
crowded room.

Hadn't he already heard everything? Certainly there was
nothing new to learn.

"We have another letter," a man up front reported.

Eliab looked up to see Seth, a short man, waving a scroll
in the air.

It could be from any of the apostles, Eliab considered as he
watched Seth unroll it. *Maybe even Paul.*

Eliab knew him well. It was Paul who convinced him
that Jesus was the Messiah.

That's when I was really happy, Eliab thought.

That's when he finally understood what it was like to be
set free from sin. Lately, though, the details of life seemed
to overshadow that feeling.

"It's just difficult," he muttered to himself.

Life seemed tedious. He worried about everything.
How could he trust God to handle his problems?

Sure, God saved me from sin, Eliab thought, *but can He
really work in my life?*

"Moses was faithful as a servant in all God's house,"
Seth read in a sure, steady voice, "testifying to what would
be said in the future."[8]

Moses? If anything could get Eliab's attention, it was the
Israelites who wandered the wilderness.

"Today, if you hear God's voice, do not harden your
hearts as you did in the rebellion, during the time of testing in the desert, where your fathers tested and tried me—
the Lord—and for forty years saw what I did."[9]

Eliab dropped his head. He knew how the Israelites had lived.

"That's why I was angry with that generation," Seth continued, "and I said, 'Their hearts are always going astray, and they have not known my ways.' So I declared on oath in my anger, 'They shall never enter my rest.'"[10]

Rest? Eliab thought. *If only I could be at rest.* But he doubted that could happen.

"See to it, brothers," Seth read, "that none of you has a sinful, unbelieving heart that turns away from the living God. We have come to share in Christ if we hold firmly till the end the confidence we had at first."[11]

How could Eliab possibly hold on to the confidence he had in the beginning? Sure, he boldly stepped out in faith, believing Jesus could cover his sins. It was obvious that God led him out of bondage. But could God conquer his everyday troubles?

"So we see that the Israelites were not able to enter, because of their unbelief," Seth went on.[12]

That's right, Eliab inwardly agreed. *They had such little faith.*

"Since the promise of entering His rest still stands," Seth said, "let us be careful that none of you be found to have fallen short of it."[13]

The promise of rest still stands? I can fall short of it?

"For if Joshua had given them rest, God would not have spoken later about another day. There remains, then, a Sabbath-rest for the people of God. For anyone who enters God's rest also rests from his own work."[14]

A Sabbath-rest?

"Let us, therefore, make every effort to enter that rest,

so that no one will fall by following their example of disobedience."[15]

Eliab's stomach sank.

Have I been following their example? Have I been faithless?

He knew Jesus saved him for eternity. But could Jesus save him today? Was He the Promise?

Is Jesus our rest? he thought.

"Come to me, all you who are weary and burdened," he whispered Jesus' words, "and I will give you rest. Take my yoke upon you and learn from me. For I am gentle and humble in heart, and you will find rest for your souls. For my yoke is easy and my burden is light."[16]

Of course, Jesus' burden is light.

Like the plowed fields and pruned vineyards of Canaan, Jesus would do the work in Eliab's life. Eliab didn't have to be anxious. He could just believe in God and enjoy the fruits of Christ's labor. It was the ultimate kind of rest.

Why had he chosen to live in the desert for so long—shaking his fruitless, barren life? He had enough faith for Jesus to redeem him, but not enough for Jesus to live through him.

God had given him the Promised Land.

But I've settled for the weary wilderness, he thought. *Not anymore.*

He looked up in the air, certain his ancestors could hear him.

"I've found Canaan," he announced. "I've found the Rest."

Therefore do not let anyone judge you by what you eat or drink, or with regard to a religious festival . . . *a Sabbath day*. These are a shadow of the things that were to come; *the reality, however, is found in Christ.*

COLOSSIANS 2:16-17

A Second Look at
The Weary's Rest

Prophecy
The Israelites set out from Rameses on the fifteenth day of the first month . . . They marched out boldly in full view of all the Egyptians. (Numbers 33:3)

> #### Fulfillment
> *We have come to share in Christ if we hold firmly till the end the confidence we had at first. (Hebrews 3:14)*

Prophecy
How often they rebelled against him in the desert and grieved him in the wasteland! . . . They did not remember his power—the day he redeemed them from the oppressor, the day he displayed his miraculous signs in Egypt. (Psalm 78:40,42-43)

> #### Fulfillment
> *So then, just as you received Christ Jesus as Lord, continue to live in him, rooted and built up in him, strengthened in the faith as you were taught. (Colossians 2:6-7)*

Prophecy
"Today, if you hear his voice, do not harden your hearts as you did in the rebellion, during the time of testing in

the desert, where your fathers tested and tried me and for
forty years saw what I did. That is why I was angry with
that generation, and I said, 'Their hearts are always going
astray, and they have not known my ways.' So I declared
on oath in my anger, 'They shall never enter my rest.'"
(Hebrews 3:7-11, quoting Psalm 95:7-11)

> ### Fulfillment
> *Therefore, since the promise of entering his rest
> still stands, let us be careful that none of you be
> found to have fallen short of it. (Hebrews 4:1)*
>
> *For if Joshua had given them rest, God would
> not have spoken later about another day. There
> remains, then, a Sabbath-rest for the people of
> God; for anyone who enters God's rest also rests
> from his own work, just as God did from his.
> Let us, therefore, make every effort to enter that
> rest, so that no one will fall by following their
> example of disobedience. (Hebrews 4:8-11)*

∞

"Come to me, all you who are weary and burdened, . . .

> "I am the vine; you are the branches. If a man
> remains in me and I in him, he will bear much fruit;
> apart from me you can do nothing."
>
> JOHN 15:5

Do not be anxious about anything, but in everything, by prayer and petition, with thanksgiving,

present your requests to God. And the peace of God, which transcends all understanding, will guard your hearts and your minds in Christ Jesus.

PHILIPPIANS 4:6-7

. . . and I will give you rest." (Matthew 11:28)

Therefore I will boast all the more gladly about my weaknesses, so that Christ's power may rest on me. That is why, for Christ's sake, I delight in weaknesses, in insults, in hardships, in persecutions, in difficulties. For when I am weak, then I am strong.

2 CORINTHIANS 12:9-10

The one who calls you is faithful and he will do it.

1 THESSALONIANS 5:24

I pray that out of his glorious riches he may strengthen you with power through his Spirit in your inner being, so that Christ may dwell in your hearts through faith.

EPHESIANS 3:16-17

∞

Discover Canaan and Jesus' rest by reading the following accounts:

Numbers 13:17–14:35 — The Israelites' Rebellion and God's Punishment

Joshua 1–2 — The New Generation and Canaan

Hebrews 3:5–4:11 — The Rest Found in Jesus

CHAPTER SEVEN

THE PRIEST AND THE OFFERING

Jesus in the Sacrificial System

A fresh coat of blood dripped from Bohan's knuckles. He watched the warm fluid stream down his hand, dribbling onto the ground.

"This is how it's done," his father said as he walked around the square altar, brushing streaks over each bronze horn. He stopped at the edge and poured the blood onto the red-stained dirt.

Bohan jerked back as it splattered.

His father grabbed his arm and pulled him forward. "Don't avoid the blood. It's your life. As I've always told you, it's God's way of making right the things you do wrong."[1]

It's not life, Bohan thought, dabbing his wet fingers onto the altar. *It's death*. The sacrificed animals were his proof. *What does he know, anyway?* Bohan rarely listened to his father. The blood lodged under his fingernails was repulsive. He avoided everything the blood represented— including his father.

"Very good," his father said.

Bohan wiped his fingers on his white robe. His father, as usual, hung his hands to his sides, letting them dry.

How can he be so calm? Bohan thought. *Doesn't the blood make him sick? Sure, as the high priest he's commanded to never mourn death. But isn't the dank smell enough to make his stomach quiver?*

His father motioned to the first man in line. "You do this one alone. Now remember, a good priest lets people take all the time they need."

Bohan watched as the man stepped toward the altar. How many times had he seen him there before? At least three since he started training.

"This sacrifice," the old man slowly said, handing Bohan a small, shaking goat, "is for my sin." He lifted a rough knife.

Bohan flinched and shut his eyes, feeling the goat's blood cover his skin.

"That's right," his father said, pushing the basin closer to the sacrifice. "Now, catch the blood like this."

Bohan quickly dropped the goat onto the crusty grate and dipped his finger into the basin. He stumbled around the vessel, smearing the blood as he went.

"When can I start learning about the rest of the tabernacle?" he asked quietly, glancing over at the holy tent. Its leather roof sank in the middle.

"Just watch the blood."

Bohan looked back at the altar. His skin crawled as his father cut the offering.

"First, you must understand the sacrifices, then you can learn the other details of worship."

Bohan watched as the old man stared at the goat and then limped away.

"The entire tabernacle," his father continued, "from what's in the tent to what's in the outer court, is very complex. It's important that you study every aspect, including the altar. After all, the tabernacle is a copy of what's in the sky. Moses was shown an exact example. If you want to know what's up there, just look down here."[2]

Surely there isn't an altar in heaven. There wouldn't be sacrifices up there.

"Are you ready for me, Zadok?" a voice called from behind him.

"Yes, yes." His father twisted around. "This is Jether. He'll continue your training today."

Bohan looked down at the man's bony ankles.

"He's the best priest we have," his father said. "Listen and learn." He turned and walked toward the holy tent.

Bohan's heart dropped. *Do I really have to continue with this?*

"Well," Jether said, stepping toward the altar. "I guess I'll just start with the basics." He paused and looked at Bohan. "I know this is hard to take. But as you learn more, you'll gain a new perspective."

He ran his palm over the vessel's wide rim. "I understand

you've already mediated a sin sacrifice. A guilt offering is the same idea. But instead of covering our unclean nature, it covers our daily wrongs."

Bohan didn't respond. His stomach was too queasy.

"Well then, let's go on to the other sacrifices." Jether squinted at the line of people. "Who here needs to make a fellowship offering?"

Bohan's face paled as he moved back from the altar. He couldn't handle one more sacrifice.

Jether glanced at him.

"Never mind," he called to those assembled. "We'll stop until after the music."

He quickly turned around.

"Bohan, I know what you're going through. I was once in training, too, you know. I felt the same way I imagine you do. But we need these sacrifices for life."

For life? Bohan thought. That's what his father always tried to explain.

"Don't you see? Our souls are dead," Jether continued. "God's glory was taken from us when Adam and Eve rebelled. The blood brings us back into fellowship with Him."

"But how?" Bohan asked, barely able to speak.

"God, you know, used the skin of an animal to cover our bare shame, right?"

Bohan nodded. He knew that God had replaced Adam's and Eve's garments of fig leaves with leather ones after they sinned.

"Well, God had to kill an animal, didn't He? A life had to be taken to cover our wrongs. The sacrifice's blood was proof that we'd been covered." Jether paused. "It still is."[3]

Bohan looked down at his red fingers.

"Your soul has been spared," Jether said, "because of the blood of another. Abel, Noah, Abraham—they all knew this. That's why they offered sacrifices."

Bohan glanced over at the altar. Suddenly he saw it in a new light. Had he been like Adam and Eve? Was he trying to cover his own wrongs instead of letting God do it?

"Let's stop for today," Jether said as the choir began to rehearse.

Bohan nodded again, his mind whirling. He made sacrifices because that's what God commanded. Could it be that God had made the first sacrifice for him? He had always thought that God was cruel. But it was really just the opposite. God used the blood to save him.

Hasn't my father ever explained this? he thought, watching Jether walk toward the tent.

"Many, O Lord, are the wonders you've done,"[4] a man sang as Bohan walked to the other side of the court. It was a psalm written by King David. "Sacrifice and offering you did not desire," the singer continued.[5]

What a strange thing for the psalm to say. Bohan leaned against a pillar. The sacrifices were his life, weren't they? That's what Jether told him. Why would God not desire them?

"But my ears you have pierced," the man sang.[6]

Only servants had pierced ears.[7] *What servant could take the place of a sacrifice?*

"Burnt offerings and sin offerings you did not require," the singer continued. "Here I am, I have come—it is written about me in the scroll."[8]

Who? Bohan thought, feeling a hand grab onto his arm.

Who is it written about?

"The psalms speak of the future," his father said, just as the music faded. "They point ahead to what's coming. A final Sacrifice will soon be here."

"A final sacrifice?" Bohan asked as he turned and looked at him.

"One day, God will no longer desire our sacrifices. A Servant's blood will take their place."

"But who would possibly die for us?"

"A Priest," his father said.

"A priest?"

"Yes, just as the psalms speak of a Servant, they tell of a Priest."

His father leaned closer.

"The Lord has sworn and will not change his mind," he recited part of a psalm. "'You are a priest forever, in the order of Melchizedek.'"[9]

But all priests were from the line of Aaron.

"Melchizedek was a priest and a king," his father said. "No one knows where he came from or where he went. When he met Abraham after battle, instead of sacrificing goats and pigeons, he offered bread and wine as if it were his own body and blood."[10]

His own blood? Bohan thought.

"The coming Priest," his father said, "will be of this same order. He won't make sacrifices. He'll offer bread and wine. He'll offer Himself."[11]

But who would do something like that? Bohan thought. *Who would climb on the altar and die for me?*

"Melchizedek is referred to as the Lord," his father said. "That's what the psalms say."[12]

"You mean God?"

"Yes." His father looked to the sky. "The One who is coming will be the Lord. The real tabernacle is up there somewhere. And the true Priest will sacrifice an offering of Himself. His eternal blood will cover us forever."

"God will use His own blood?"

"He will," his father said. "It's been His plan all along. The sacrifices are merely a sign of what's in the future. They're a temporary solution until the real Sacrifice can come."

Bohan looked to the sky. He could almost see the altar. *Is the Holy Priest really there, waiting to be the Final Offering? Will God kill Himself, as He did the animals, to cover our bare shame—to bring us into fellowship?*

"Just keep your eyes on the blood," his father said. "It covers you now. And later, it will save you forever."

For the first time, Bohan really heard what his father said. He slowly reached out and touched the stains on his father's hand. Then he looked down at his own blood-soiled robe. And despite the spots, he had never felt cleaner.

[Jesus] has become *a high priest forever,* in the order of *Melchizedek.*

HEBREWS 6:20

Because *Jesus* lives forever, he has a permanent priesthood . . . He *sacrificed for [our] sins* once for all when *he offered himself.*

HEBREWS 7:24,27

A SECOND LOOK AT
The Priest and the Offering

PROPHECY

"Then have them make a sanctuary for me . . . Make this tabernacle and all its furnishings exactly like the pattern I will show you." (Exodus 25:8-9)

Fulfillment
[Priests] serve at a sanctuary that is a copy and a shadow of what is in heaven. This is why Moses was warned when he was about to build the tabernacle: "See to it that you make every-thing according to the pattern shown you on the mountain." (Hebrews 8:5)

PROPHECY

Sacrifice and offering you did not desire, but my ears you have pierced; burnt offerings and sin offerings you did not require. Then I said, "Here I am, I have come—it is written about me in the scroll." (Psalm 40:6-7)

Fulfillment
God presented [Jesus] as a sacrifice of atone-ment, through faith in his blood. (Romans 3:25)

PROPHECY

The LORD says to my Lord: "Sit at my right hand until I make your enemies a footstool for your feet." . . . The LORD has sworn and will not change his mind: "You are a priest forever, in the order of Melchizedek." (Psalm 110:1,4)

> *Fulfillment*
> *[Jesus] has become a high priest forever, in the order of Melchizedek. (Hebrews 6:20)*

───────
∞

Without the shedding of blood . . .

> The blood of goats and bulls and the ashes of a heifer sprinkled on those who are ceremonially unclean sanctify them so that they are outwardly clean. How much more, then, will the blood of Christ, who through the eternal Spirit offered himself unblemished to God, cleanse our consciences from acts that lead to death.
>
> HEBREWS 9:13-14

. . . there is no forgiveness. (Hebrews 9:22)

> We have one who speaks to the Father in our defense—Jesus Christ, the Righteous One. He is the atoning sacrifice for our sins.
>
> 1 JOHN 2:1-2

But because Jesus lives forever, he has a permanent priesthood. Therefore he is able to save completely those who come to God through him, because he always lives to intercede for them ... Unlike the other high priests, he does not need to offer sacrifices day after day, first for his own sins, and then for the sins of the people. He sacrificed for their sins once for all when he offered himself.

HEBREWS 7:24-25,27

This is love: not that we loved God, but that he loved us and sent his Son as an atoning sacrifice for our sins.

1 JOHN 4:10

For there is one God and one mediator between God and men, the man Christ Jesus, who gave himself as a ransom for all men.

1 TIMOTHY 2:5-6

For this reason [Jesus] had to be made like his brothers in every way, in order that he might become a merciful and faithful high priest in service to God, and that he might make atonement for the sins of the people.

HEBREWS 2:17

∞

Focus on the final Priest and His blood:
    Exodus 27:1-8 — The Altar
    Leviticus 1–9 — The Sacrifices and Priests

Hebrews 7:23–8:6; 10:1-14 — The Priest and Offering
   of Jesus Christ
Genesis 14:17-20; Hebrews 6:19–7:22 — Melchizedek

CHAPTER EIGHT

THE REFUGE

Jesus in the Cities of Refuge
and in Isaiah 53

O zni stepped on the front edge of the man's sandal and shoved him.

"Don't fall," he whispered, pulling his foot away. The man stumbled to the other side of the path. His ankle twisted as he fell into the arms of Barkos.

"Back so soon?" Barkos said. He let out a sour chuckle. Ozni could almost smell his friend's breath from across the pathway. His stomach turned at the stale scent of cheap wine.

Barkos pushed the man again. His head bobbed up and down with heavy wheezes.

"It's all right," Ozni said as he clutched the man's trembling arm. "Isn't that right, boys?" he yelled to his companions standing on the edge of the path. "It only *feels* like

Barkos's breath will kill him. But it hasn't killed *us* yet."

The young men threw back their heads in cackling howls. They had spent many afternoons at this spot in the road tormenting those who passed by. This man was an especially easy target; they'd been teasing him since they were children.

"Oh, cut it out," Barkos yelled. "Just push him back to me."

Ozni thrust out his arms. The man tripped, staggering to the far side of the road.

"He's gonna fall," someone shouted. "He's going down."

The man's feet wobbled on the edge. He teetered and tumbled over the cliff.

Ozni forced a dry swallow and glanced at Barkos. They both raced to the ledge, the others only a few steps behind them.

"We teased him too much this time," Ozni said as they wound down the mountain. "He's too short and skinny for that."

They stopped at the edge of another drop-off. Ozni's foot slid. He squatted and grabbed onto a stiff bush, looking out over the ridge.

"Here he is!" Ozni called. He dropped to his knees, then his stomach. "His robe is caught around his neck. He's hanging from a tree." Ozni reached out for the strands of brown hair knotted around a branch. "I can't get to him."

Small rocks scraped his arms as he scooted his chest further over the edge.

"Father," he heard the man gasp, "forgive them. They don't know what they're doing."[1]

"Are you all right?" Ozni said.

The man didn't answer; his body twitched and then hung limp.

"Just grunt if you're still alive."

Only the sound of a rolling rock broke the stillness.

"He's dead," Barkos called.

"No!" Ozni scrambled to his feet.

"He is," Barkos said. "And even if he weren't, there's no way we could get him off that tree. Face it—we've killed him."

"But we didn't mean to." Ozni spun around. "Didn't you hear him? He said we didn't know what we were doing. He said we were innocent."

"Tell it to his avenger," Barkos snapped, "before he kills you."

"Don't talk about that." Ozni's skin tingled with fear.

"The avenger will be his father." Barkos turned and began to stumble up the steep hill. "He has no brother to avenge his death."

Ozni's hands went cold; he didn't move.

"Come on," Barkos screamed, "let's get out of here."

Ozni knew Barkos was right. The man was dead. He took one last look and then scrambled up the mountain.

"We could run to a city of refuge," he blurted out. "We could plead our case to the priests."

"Are you crazy?" Barkos hissed. "There's nothing that can save us but ourselves."

"But we could run to Hebron," Ozni said. "It's the closest city of refuge."

"You're guilty," Barkos shouted. "No one is going to give you refuge. You're a fool if you think so." He climbed onto the road. "There's no such thing as undeserved forgiveness."

"Then I'll go alone," Ozni said as he hurried up behind him.

Barkos swung around and yelled, "You'll never be able to save yourself."

❧

Ozni ran for a long time and didn't look back. He just followed the twisted path, wiping his sticky hair from his forehead and the beaded sweat from his lip.

"Refuge," he groaned, reading a stone pillar. He followed it, veering to the left as the road split in two directions. "I can get there."

His heart pounded in his ears. *It's not just the running that makes it throb,* he thought. *It's all the sin inside of me.*

He turned a sharp corner and continued to weave down the long, wide road.

"Hebron," he said, finally seeing the top of its main gate. The white rock looked brown in the setting of the sun. "I've killed a man," he called as he stumbled to the entrance and walked through the stone corridor. "Please save me." He fell to his knees.

"We have a manslayer here," someone shouted, pulling Ozni to his feet. "A manslayer has arrived."

Ozni crumpled with fatigue. He could hear footsteps pounding all around him.

"My name is Moza," the man said. "I'm Hebron's senior priest."

Ozni watched his frizzy beard swing across his chest.

"This refuge will be your protection," Moza said, raising

his voice. "That is, if you're innocent—if you committed this crime accidentally."

The sound of shuffling feet stopped. Ozni eyed the small crowd now assembled.

"But if you killed someone with malice," Moza went on, "we must leave you outside the gate. You'll have to face the judgment of the avenger alone."

Ozni's throat tightened as if the avenger's hands were already choking his weak neck.

"I'm innocent," he said, his voice cracking. "I caused a man to hang from a tree. But as he hung there dying, he asked his father to forgive me and said that I did not know what I was doing."

Murmurs swept through the crowd.

"He said I didn't know what I was doing," Ozni yelled, wobbling, then regaining his balance. "He called me innocent, ignorant in my actions."

"How odd," Moza interrupted. "A dying man interceding for a manslayer?"

"I know," Ozni said, "but his testimony's the only thing I've got. I was mean and cruel. Yet the dying man, he called me innocent. I know I don't deserve it. Still, that's what he said."

Moza turned and walked over to several men standing at the front of the crowd. They whispered and shook their heads, looking occasionally at Ozni.

"Well," Moza finally said, "we've come to a very unusual decision. Since the man you wronged called you innocent, you'll be allowed to stay in this refuge."

Ozni's knees collapsed. Moza reached out and grabbed his arm.

"Thank you," Ozni said, scanning the crowd.

"I know you're exhausted," Moza said. "You'll stay at my house tonight. Later we'll find you a place of your own." He loosened his grip. "Can you walk?"

"I think so."

"I'm right next to you if you need me," Moza said.

They slowly made their way down a hill. Ozni could hardly see in front of him.

"Are you a Jew?" Moza asked.

Ozni nodded.

"That's what I thought. The refuge, though, saves everyone. Jews, Gentiles—it doesn't matter."[2]

A bridge, arching over a wide stream, was just a few paces ahead. Ozni stared at the water shining with the moon.

"And your name?" Moza asked.

"Ozni." The bridge creaked as he stepped onto it.

"Well, Ozni, can you read?"

"Enough to get by."

"Can you write?"

"Hardly at all." Ozni grabbed onto the railing.

"Well, that's good enough," Moza said. "You can be my assistant. You'll start tomorrow."

A priest's assistant? His friends would have laughed at the silly idea.

"That's my house," Moza said, pointing to a square structure in the middle of the field. "It's not much, but it's enough for us." He looked at Ozni. "Do you have family?"

"Yes," Ozni said, "a wife but no children."

"Well, for now, the refuge gives you salvation," Moza said, as he walked up and put his hand on the door's flimsy knob. "But when a high priest dies, you'll be given ultimate freedom. You'll be able to go home. The avenger can no longer judge you."

Moza pushed open the door; it squeaked as it swung. Ozni stepped inside.

"Everyone's asleep," Moza whispered. "I'll show you your room."

They walked past a few chairs and a skinny table. Moza reached down and picked up an oil lamp. Ozni followed him until they stopped in front of a coarse linen curtain.

"I think you'll have everything you need," Moza said as he pushed it back. He walked inside the room and lit a candlestick with the flame on his lamp. "I'm glad you've been saved. There's no condemnation for those in the refuge." He turned and left.

As his footsteps faded, Ozni fell onto the lumpy cushion. Pulling his damp robe from his body, he flung it to the floor.

"Barkos," he whispered, "I wonder what's happened to you?" He cringed, knowing the answer.

He rolled over onto his back and closed his eyes.

❧

The morning sun woke Ozni. Outside his window he could hear Moza feeding the chickens.

Pulling his robe over his tunic, Ozni pushed back the curtain. He held his aching side, massaging it as he shuffled into the house's main room.

"My wife left some figs and bread on the table for you," Moza greeted as he came back inside. "After you eat, we'll begin our work." He pointed to a cave across the field. "Meet me there when you can."

Ozni stopped by the door, grabbing four figs and a fat loaf of bread. By the time he reached the cave, he had swallowed the figs almost whole and eaten the entire loaf.

"Come in, come in," Moza called.

The air inside the cave was considerably cooler. Ozni walked toward a small light.

"Sit here." Moza pointed to a narrow stool. "And get comfortable. We'll be awhile."

The bumpy wood dug into Ozni's thighs. He took a deep breath, tasting the cave's musty smell.

"Just let me finish this one word," Moza said, scribbling an inky reed over a thin animal hide.

Ozni glanced up at the rows of animal skins hanging from the dark ceiling and then back at the one on the table.

"Perfect," Moza said, pulling his reed from the hide and dropping it into a clay cup of ink. "Aren't the words of Isaiah just perfect?"

"Who?" Ozni asked.

"You know, the prophet Isaiah."

"Oh yes, of course," Ozni said. But he had never read any of Isaiah's writings. He'd only heard about his predictions.

"Ever since Isaiah died, we've been copying down his words so that others can understand them." Moza reached over and picked up a thick leather scroll. He pushed it toward Ozni. "Since you said you could read, I'll have you recite these passages so I can write them."

Ozni glanced at the black smudges covering Moza's hands and then grabbed the scroll.

"We'll begin with Isaiah's description of the Servant."

"Oh, I've heard of him before," Ozni said. "People say he's coming to rescue us from our enemies."

"Well, that depends on which enemy you're talking about."

Ozni felt his eyebrows press toward the top of his nose. Everyone knew that Israel's worst enemy was the Assyrians.

"God's Servant won't rescue us from our physical enemies," Moza said. "He'll save us from the enemy of God's wrath." He looked down at the scroll stretched across the table. "It's right here. It says that the Servant will bear the sin of many and make intercession for the transgressors. The Lord will lay bare His holy arm and all the earth will see the salvation of our God."[3]

Ozni's stool creaked as he scooted forward.

"The Servant will be the Arm—the Hand of God," Moza said. "He'll save us from God's judgment of our sinful hearts."

"An arm?" Ozni mumbled. "God will send his arm to save us from his judgment?" He paused. "God will send himself to save us from himself?"

"Yes," Moza said, "precisely." He leaned closer. "The Servant will be like this refuge. He'll redeem those running for their lives."

"But the refuge only saves innocent men," Ozni said.

"I know. That's what's so brilliant about God's plan. The Servant will take our wrongs upon Himself. And because He takes our judgment, He can declare all people innocent. Everyone will be saved who comes to Him."

"Everyone?" Ozni asked. *Even me?* he wondered. His heart, he was sure, was more sinful than others. After all, he had killed a man.

"Yes, everyone," Moza said. "The cities of refuge, all six of them, are an example of what's coming. They point to the Servant. He will be the seventh and ultimate City of Refuge. Just like the seventh day of the week, He'll be the final Salvation."

Ozni couldn't help but think of his own plight.

"Many people won't run to the Refuge," Moza continued. "They won't believe the Servant can save them or that God will give them grace. They'll think they can rescue themselves by outwitting the Father."

Ozni felt his heart begin to pound.

"You, of all people, should understand this," Moza said softly. "The refuge gave you physical mercy from the avenger. But one day, the true Refuge will save us all from the Father's wrath."

"But how will we recognize this refuge?" Ozni asked.

Moza motioned over to the scroll, still partly rolled up in Ozni's hands.

Ozni quickly pulled it open.

"Start from there." Moza pointed to a line in the middle.

Ozni cleared his throat.

"He had no beauty or majesty to attract us to him," he read, squinting at the words, "nothing in his appearance that we should desire him. He was despised and rejected by men, a man of sorrows, and familiar with suffering."[4]

He stopped reading and looked at Moza.

"Go on. Go on," Moza said.

"Surely he took up our infirmities and carried our sorrows, yet we considered him stricken by God, smitten by him, and afflicted. But he was pierced for our transgressions, he was crushed for our iniquities; the punishment that brought us peace was upon him, and by his wounds we are healed."[5]

Ozni kept his head down and skimmed the rest of the words.

"It says that he'll be like a lamb led to slaughter, but he won't open his mouth. He'll be cut off from the living and given a grave with the wicked and the rich, even though he does nothing wrong."[6]

Ozni rested the scroll against the table.

"He will be like a guilt offering. And after he suffers, he'll once again see life."[7]

A breeze blew into the cave. The candle's flame flickered, growing tall and wide as it swirled.

"I know how thankful you are that your life has been saved," Moza said. "But do you want your soul to be saved, too?"

"Of course," Ozni said.

"Then you must run to the final Refuge."

Ozni closed his eyes. It sounded so simple.

"Whenever you see someone who's despised," Moza said, slowly, "a man who heals the sick; who's pierced and crushed but doesn't open His mouth; who's led to slaughter; who's killed with the wicked and the rich."

Ozni opened his eyes.

"And who dies on an altar for sinners," he interrupted, "who comes back to life to justify everyone—no matter if they're a Jew or a Gentile, then we'll know it's Him."

Ozni took a deep breath and reverently ran his fingers over the scroll.

"Surely, all of us will run to Him," he said, looking at Moza. He smiled. "Surely, we'll all run to the Refuge."

So God has given us
both his promise and
his oath . . . Therefore,
*we who have fled to
him for refuge* can
take *new courage.*

HEBREWS 6:18 (NLT)

A Second Look at
The Refuge

Prophecy

"Six of the towns you give the Levites will be cities of refuge, to which a person who has killed someone may flee." (Numbers 35:6) . . . This is the rule concerning the man who kills another and flees there to save his life— one who kills his neighbor unintentionally, without malice aforethought. (Deuteronomy 19:4)

Fulfillment

At one time we too were foolish, disobedient, deceived and enslaved by all kinds of passions and pleasures. We lived in malice and envy, being hated and hating one another. But when the kindness and love of God our Savior appeared, he saved us, not because of righteous things we had done, but because of his mercy . . . so that, having been justified by his grace, we might become heirs having the hope of eternal life. (Titus 3:3-5,7)

Even though I was once a blasphemer and a persecutor and a violent man, I was shown mercy because I acted in ignorance and unbelief. The grace of our Lord was poured out on me abundantly, along with the faith and love that are in Christ Jesus. (1 Timothy 1:13-14)

Jesus said, "Father, forgive them, for they do not know what they are doing." (Luke 23:34)

PROPHECY

"These six towns will be a place of refuge for Israelites, aliens and any other people living among them, so that anyone who has killed another accidentally can flee there." (Numbers 35:15)

Fulfillment

Here there is no Greek or Jew, circumcised or uncircumcised, barbarian, Scythian, slave or free, but Christ is all, and is in all. (Colossians 3:11)

PROPHECY

"The assembly must protect the one accused of murder from the avenger of blood and send him back to the city of refuge to which he fled. He must stay there until the death of the high priest, who was anointed with the holy oil." (Numbers 35:25)

Fulfillment

Therefore, holy brothers, who share in the heavenly calling, fix your thoughts on Jesus, the apostle and high priest whom we confess. (Hebrews 3:1)

PROPHECY

He was despised and rejected by men. (Isaiah 53:3)

Fulfillment
He came to that which was his own, but his own did not receive him. (John 1:11)

PROPHECY
Surely he took up our infirmities and carried our sorrows. (Isaiah 53:4)

Fulfillment
When evening came, many who were demon-possessed were brought to him, and he drove out the spirits with a word and healed all the sick. (Matthew 8:16)

PROPHECY
But he was pierced for our transgressions, he was crushed for our iniquities; the punishment that brought us peace was upon him, and by his wounds we are healed. We all, like sheep, have gone astray, each of us has turned to his own way; and the LORD has laid on him the iniquity of us all. (Isaiah 53:5-6)

Fulfillment
To this you were called, because Christ suffered for you . . . He himself bore our sins in his body on the tree, so that we might die to sins and live for righteousness; by his wounds you have been healed. For you were like sheep going astray, but now you have returned to the Shepherd and Overseer of your souls. (1 Peter 2:21,24-25)

PROPHECY

He was led like a lamb to the slaughter, and as a sheep before her shearers is silent, so he did not open his mouth. (Isaiah 53:7)

Fulfillment

When he was accused by the chief priests and the elders, he gave no answer. Then Pilate asked him, "Don't you hear the testimony they are bringing against you?" But Jesus made no reply, not even to a single charge. (Matthew 27:12-14)

PROPHECY

By oppression and judgment he was taken away. (Isaiah 53:8)

Fulfillment

Then Pilate took Jesus and had him flogged. The soldiers twisted together a crown of thorns and put it on his head. (John 19:1-2)

PROPHECY

He was assigned a grave with the wicked, and with the rich in his death. (Isaiah 53:9)

Fulfillment

*Two robbers were crucified with him, one on his right and one on his left.
(Matthew 27:38)*

As evening approached, there came a rich man from Arimathea, named Joseph . . . Going to

*Pilate, he asked for Jesus' body, and Pilate
ordered that it be given to him. Joseph took the
body, wrapped it in clean linen cloth, and placed
it in his own new tomb.
(Matthew 27:57-60)*

PROPHECY
Yet it was the LORD's will to crush him and cause him
to suffer, and though the LORD makes his life a guilt
offering, he will see his offspring and prolong his days.
(Isaiah 53:10)

> *Fulfillment*
> *For what the law was powerless to do in that it
> was weakened by the sinful nature, God did by
> sending his own Son in the likeness of sinful
> man to be a sin offering. And so he condemned
> sin in sinful man, in order that the righteous
> requirements of the law might be fully met in us.
> (Romans 8:3-4)*

PROPHECY
After the suffering of his soul, he will see the light of life
and be satisfied; by his knowledge my righteous servant
will justify many, and he will bear their iniquities. (Isaiah
53:11)

> *Fulfillment*
> *He was delivered over to death for our sins and
> was raised to life for our justification.
> (Romans 4:25)*

∞

Therefore, there is now no condemnation . . .

> For he has rescued us from the dominion of darkness
> and brought us into the kingdom of the Son he
> loves, in whom we have redemption, the forgiveness
> of sins.
>
> COLOSSIANS 1:13-14

. . . for those who are in Christ Jesus. (Romans 8:1)

> Then Jesus cried out . . . "For I did not come to
> judge the world, but to save it."
>
> JOHN 12:44,47

> But because of his great love for us, God, who is rich
> in mercy, made us alive with Christ even when we
> were dead in transgressions — it is by grace you have
> been saved.
>
> EPHESIANS 2:4-5

> For all have sinned and fall short of the glory of God,
> and are justified freely by his grace through the
> redemption that came by Christ Jesus.
>
> ROMANS 3:23-24

> Therefore, since we have been justified through faith,
> we have peace with God through our Lord Jesus
> Christ, through whom we have gained access by faith
> into this grace in which we now stand.
>
> ROMANS 5:1-2

Then Jesus declared . . . "whoever comes to me I will
never drive away."

JOHN 6:35,37

∽

Take a deeper look at how everyone can escape judgment
and flee for salvation:

Numbers 35:6-28; Deuteronomy 19:1-13; Joshua
20 — The Cities of Refuge
Isaiah 53 — The Saving Servant

CHAPTER NINE

THE CHILD

Jesus in the Messianic Bloodline

Ochus reached up to the night sky and covered a sparkling star with the tip of his finger.

How small they are, he thought as he released it and watched its light once again scatter over the darkness.

He leaned back onto the grassy hill and examined the other suspended dots. A tarnished one slipped from where it hung and tumbled down the sky, nearly landing on the priests' tall and skinny palace.

If only I could catch it, he imagined.

But that would be impossible. Like all falling stars, it had probably drifted somewhere beyond his reach—out across the horizon.

He glanced over at the palace. Shadows of magi raced across the candlelit rooms. He watched the men scramble to the third-floor balcony.

"You missed it," he whispered as they scoured the spotted sky. That's why he studied in the meadow. He could see everything from there.

But soon, he'd no longer be an apprentice. He'd be a true magus.

"Then I'll have to study in that stuffy mansion."

He threw his sheepskin ball to the sky and pretended to bounce it off the moon. There was so much he didn't understand about the heavens. At times, the stars seemed like holes in an enormous black canopy.

They're like a window into another world, he thought.

But the official magi had their own theories. Zara, his instructor, often paced before him, expounding his long-winded philosophies.

It doesn't matter what I think.

Even though his father was one of the best stargazers in Persia, Ochus still had to earn his place within the priestly caste.[1]

How can I? he thought.

Reading the stars was confusing. And besides, could they really tell of the past and the future? Surely, the sky could speak of only one thing.

"Its Creator," he said softly as he closed his eyes.

His skin tingled with a burning heat. It was as if the sky had suddenly caught on fire. He jerked open his eyes, squinting up at a mass of light hovering over the western horizon.

"What is it?" he gasped, jumping to his feet.

He watched the light teeter, shooting streaks of red and green over the heavens.

"It's like a royal crown." He grabbed his leather ball and

stumbled toward the palace. "Yes, that's it. Of course, it's
like a royal crown."

He ran down the hill, tripping as he watched the brilliant rays.

"The star. It's the Jews' star."

For years he'd tried to imagine what it would look like.
The Jews never described it—only that it would announce
the birth of their king.

"Your messiah is here," he yelled.

Finally, the Jewish ruler had arrived. How long had they
waited? At first, the Jews thought He'd come to save them
from the Babylonians. But it was the Persians who set them
free from captivity. When Greece conquered the land, the
Jews still waited for their Savior. Even those who didn't
return to their homeland, but stayed in Persia, believed a
ruler would eventually come to save Israel.

Now, Ochus figured, scrambling into the palace, *he's
come to conquer the Romans.*

He ran up the stairs, through the murky hallway, and
climbed another story to the balcony.

Ever since the Jews settled in Persia, the magi had kept
watch for the heavenly phenomena. They never worshiped
the Jewish Lord. After all, the priests were too busy prac-
ticing magic and astrology.[2]

But what astrologer can resist a star? Ochus thought,
rushing to the side of the balcony and staring to the sky.

"A star will come out of Jacob," he recited. "A scepter
will rise out of Israel."[3]

How many times had he heard that Jewish prophecy?

The Jews believed it spoke of their coming ruler. It
predicted he would one day be born under a star as a

descendant of the Hebrew patriarch named Jacob.

"Ochus," a voice called behind him. He spun around.

Cyrus, one of his favorite magi, stood several paces away. His small frame all but disappeared in his oversized robe.

"Can you believe it's here?" Cyrus said, smiling. He surveyed the sky. "Zara ordered us to be here by daybreak." He looked back at Ochus. "You, Thorn, and I will leave tomorrow for Jerusalem. We must pay our respects to the Jewish king."

"Really?" Ochus couldn't believe his good fortune.

Would he really stand before the world's newest ruler? He dreamed of such an adventure. The closest he'd ever come to leaving Persia was in his imagination.

"But what about my lessons?" he asked. "Is Zara coming, too?"

That would ruin his whole journey. How could he listen to Zara's dull rhetoric for such a long trip?

"Of course he's coming," Cyrus said. "And he chose you to be our assistant. That way, you can keep up with your studies."

"What's there to study?" Ochus looked up to the sky. "The stars are just an expression of something else. They're like precious gems dangling from the robe of a king."

Cyrus let out a restricted laugh. "There goes your imagination again." He grinned as he turned to leave. "Don't let Zara hear you say that. I'll see you in the morning."

❧

At dawn, the sun sat on the distant plains. Ochus felt his side stiffen as he stood. The palace's balcony lacked the

comfort of the fields. But at least he was able to sleep. He
bent down and grabbed his robe, then startled.

"The star." He frantically scanned the sky. "Where's the
star?"

Finally, he saw its hazy outline.

"Good, you're here." Zara's distinct voice boomed across
the balcony.

Ochus whirled about.

"Now, where's everyone else?" Zara asked.

"Well," Ochus said, "I'm sure they'll be here soon."

Zara ducked under the palace's doorway, missing the
top by the length of his short, gray hair. As with everything else, he was precise in measuring just how much he
needed to stoop.

"We'll need to bring gold and frankincense," Cyrus
called from inside the palace.

"Oh yes, and we can't forget to bring the myrrh," Zara
added.

"Myrrh is for dead people," a voice shouted from
behind them.

Ochus felt the balcony tremble with Thorn's offbeat
footsteps.

"They bury people wrapped in that stuff. The Jewish
king doesn't want myrrh," Thorn said.

Why does Thorn have to come? Ochus thought. *Zara
is bad enough. Now I have to deal with Thorn's rude
comments.*

It was no secret, though, why Zara picked him. He was
the biggest of all the magi. Thieves would avoid their cara-
van as long as Thorn was around.

"Myrrh is an appropriate gift," Zara said, turning and

walking toward the door. "It's expensive and rare. What else could a king want?"

❧

It was nightfall by the time Ochus had loaded all the camels. He packed the gold, along with the other gifts, securely in small bags. How meager they seemed for a king.

But what else do you give such a mighty ruler? Ochus thought. *Nothing would be enough. After all, he's going to save the Jews.*

"Keep your eyes on the star," Zara commanded as they rode from the palace.

How could he look away?

Cyrus whistled the same song over and over during the first part of their journey. No one seemed to mind — except Thorn.

"Can't you think of another tune?" he complained. "I've been hearing that for weeks."

But who was counting? Ochus had lost track of time.

The camels never even showed signs of how long they'd been walking. They always put one callused foot in front of the other. The sharp rocks and thorny grass never detoured them.

The only thing that bothers them, Ochus thought, *is Thorn.* He could tell because his camel continually spit balls of slime onto Thorn's back.

Sure, it wasn't nice. *But what can I do?*

Thankfully, he never heard Zara preaching about the sky — except when they stopped for breaks. Ochus was far enough behind that he could ignore Zara's dull comments.

Thorn, though, didn't have an option.

"We'll stay the night here," Zara said one evening as they stopped at a small inn.

"Finally," Ochus mumbled, sliding off his camel.

They usually slept outside under tents. But the taverns were so much more exciting. Many of the guests had traveled to such places as Egypt.

"Ochus," Zara ordered, "you're not to talk to those wandering men tonight. After you unload the bags, I want you to study the sky and report your findings to me."

"Yes sir." Ochus shrugged as he turned back to the camels.

I don't mind studying the sky, he thought as Zara and the others walked to the inn. *But he doesn't really want to hear what I find.*

He tugged on a couple of bags and then looked to the sky. "My chores will have to wait," he whispered as they tumbled to the ground.

He flopped onto one of them and stared at the giant star, pulling a loaf of bread from his sack. The camels began to moan as he tossed dry chunks into his mouth.

"I'll feed you guys in a bit," he consoled, never taking his eyes off the enormous light.

How did the ancient Jews know that a star would tell of their king? he thought. *After all, they predicted it thousands of years ago.*

And it wasn't the only prophecy that told of the coming ruler. The Jewish scriptures were full of them.

"The scepter will not depart from Judah," Ochus said as he stood and gathered the bags, "nor the ruler's staff from between his feet."[4]

Judah was the son of Jacob. The savior would come from this line—the same line as King David.

"'The days are coming,'" Ochus continued, dragging the bags to the door, "'when I will raise up to David a righteous Branch, a King who will reign wisely and do what is just and right in the land.'"[5]

He dropped the bags at the entrance.

"What did the heavens say tonight?" Zara said, standing at the doorway.

"Well," Ochus avoided his stare. "Nothing has really changed from what you said today. Your lecture was profound."

Zara smiled.

"Very good," he said. "Now get some sleep. We still have a long journey."

❧

As time passed, the star kept leading. It ducked behind hills and sank into valleys, but traces of its light always remained on the surrounding sky.

"Have you heard about the king?" Zara asked weary travelers.

But all of them shrugged and kept walking.

"They have eyes to see the star," Cyrus said. "Yet their hearts have failed them."

Surely, they were just trying to survive under Rome's heavy hand.

Finally, Herod's palace slowly began to emerge on the distant horizon. It sat high on a hill, seeming to soar over Jerusalem.

"We're here," Ochus yelled, nudging his camel to move faster.

Zara led them through the narrow eastern gate.

"The palace is that way," Thorn shouted.

"We won't be going there." Zara turned his camel toward the center of town. "I want to talk to the people."

"But aren't kings found in castles?" Thorn inquired.

Zara didn't respond. Who could argue? Kings *always* lived in castles.

But surely this one wouldn't be in Herod's palace. Obviously the new king was a threat to Herod's throne. After all, Herod was not from the Jewish royal line, and it was Rome, not Israel, that bestowed on him the title of king.[6]

This new ruler, Ochus thought, *is what Herod can never be.*

The city street was crowded with carts and donkeys as Zara questioned countless men. Ochus leaned back against his camel and rested his eyes.

"Your presence is requested at the palace," he heard a voice address him in a secretive tone.

"What?" Ochus opened his eyes and looked face-to-face at a short man standing next to him.

"You and those men are looking for the Jewish king, aren't you?" the man said, fiddling with several gold rings wrapped around his fingers.

Ochus nodded.

"Well then, the governor has requested to see you."

"Governor Herod the Great?"

"Yes," the man said as Zara and the others gathered around. "I think you have something Herod wants."

Ochus felt his stomach tighten as he reached back and grabbed the reins of his camel. *What do we have that Herod wants? Unless he thinks we have the king.*

"Come with me," the man motioned.

They all scurried behind him.

"Don't touch anything," the man said once they stepped inside the castle.

Each wall was covered with gold and ivory. Marble statues lined the rooms and cedar woodworking adorned every entryway.

"Wait here." The man motioned to a marble bench. He pulled on a jewel-studded door and disappeared behind it.

Ochus tapped his foot as he watched the sun's beams crawl down his body and whirl at his feet.

"Herod will see you now," the man said, finally peeking through the door.

Zara stood first. Ochus, Cyrus, and Thorn quickly followed. At the far end of the high-ceilinged room, five vast steps led to a giant throne. A stocky man stood silently with his back to them.

"So," the man called as they walked toward him, "you're looking for the king of the Jews."

"Yes," Zara said. "We've come to worship him."

The man spun around, then paced in front of the elevated throne, his hands so tightly held together that his fingertips were deathly white.

"I'm Herod the Great." He glanced up to a nearby window. "And I've been told you think the star is this king's birth announcement."

"Well, Hebrew prophecy says that a star will come out of Jacob and a scepter . . ."

"I know what the prophecy says," Herod snapped.

He clapped his hands and watched several men hurry from hidden corners of the room.

"Show me that scroll again," he said.

A bushy-haired man dropped a thick scroll into Herod's hands. The wrinkles in the king's forehead deepened as he quickly scanned it.

"Now read it to them." He shoved it back into the man's arms.

"For this is what the prophet Micah wrote over six hundred years ago," the man said, stepping forward.

"Just read the prophecy," Herod demanded.

"But you, Bethlehem, in the land of Judah," the man read, "are by no means least among the rulers. For out of you will come a ruler who will be the shepherd of my people Israel."[7]

"Did you hear that?" Herod shouted. "The ruler—the one said to be born under that star—is to come from Bethlehem!"

Why didn't I know that? Ochus thought. He prided himself on knowing Hebrew prophecies. *But I've never heard that one.*

"What a meager town," Herod said. "It's just over the hill, on the fringes of Jerusalem. The big king will come from that puny place." He didn't attempt to hide his snicker as he strutted toward his throne.

"I'd like to ask you a favor." He sat down in the oversized chair. "Just like you, I want to go worship this king. But I can't find him." He paused, taking a sip of wine. "Go to Bethlehem and search for him. And when you find him, come tell me so that I may go as well."[8]

"It would be our honor," Zara said, bowing.

What? Ochus frowned as he backed away. *Herod's not going to worship the king. Is Zara crazy?*

"Good," Herod thundered as they pulled open the massive door. "I'll wait for your return."

"I don't trust that man," Ochus whispered once the door banged shut.

"Neither do I," Zara said as he turned and marched down the long corridor. Ochus tried to avoid his teacher's flapping robe.

Once outside, they couldn't help but see the star, now brighter than ever. It seemed so close—as if it had been knocking on the palace door.

"Let's go," Zara said, climbing onto his camel.

They hurried down the hill toward the dim lights of Bethlehem. Maybe a castle was hidden somewhere they couldn't see.

The star stopped above a small house. Ochus squinted at its clay walls. *This can't be it.*

But the star didn't move. Its brilliant beams shot downward, lighting up the shabby structure.

"Get the gifts," Zara said, dismounting his camel.

Ochus grabbed the bags of gold and spices, then hurried after him and the other magi.

The door was slightly open. Zara pushed on it.

"For to us a child is born, to us a son is given," a man's voice spilled out from the one and only room. "The government will be on his shoulders. And he will be called Wonderful Counselor, Mighty God, Everlasting Father, Prince of Peace."[9]

Ochus bumped into Cyrus, trying to get a better view.

"Watch it," Zara said.

One by one, they tumbled into the house.

"Excuse us." Zara straightened his crooked sash.

The young man bolted to his feet.

"Don't be alarmed," Zara said. "We're here to worship the king."

Ochus glanced at the other side of the room. A peasant girl sat in a rickety chair, a baby in her arms.

The king? Is it really the king?

"Come in," the man invited.

Ochus felt a mouse scurry over his feet.

"My name is Joseph and this is my wife, Mary."

Zara grabbed the bags from Ochus.

"We've brought gifts for your king," he said, handing Joseph the leather sacks.

"Gold," he said, "is for the mightiest of rulers. And myrrh. Well, myrrh is . . . "

"They bury people with it," Thorn blurted out.

"Yes." Zara cleared his throat as he bowed and stepped away. "It's very costly."

"Thank you," Mary said. "How thoughtful."

"Well, it's from Persia," Zara said. "That's where we're from. We're magi. Some call us stargazers, and we followed the star that told of your king."

"I've heard of you," Joseph said. "You're magicians and astrologers. The prophet Daniel once called you 'the wise men.'"[10]

"We've certainly been called that," Zara said, trying to conceal an arrogant grin.

Wise men? Ochus thought as the room became silent. *We're not wise.*

"Would you like to hold the baby?" Mary extended the child toward Ochus.

"The king?" he said. "Oh no, I couldn't."

Mary stood and gently placed the baby into his arms.

"He was born to be held," she assured him. "His name is Jesus. It means 'the Lord saves.'[11] He'll save you from your sins. That's what the angel told us."[12]

From my sins? Ochus thought, feeling the baby reach up and grab his finger.

"Yes," Joseph said, "we're from Jacob's bloodline. Jesus is the one the prophets said would come."[13]

"But isn't he here to fight your enemies?" Ochus interjected.

Joseph smiled.

"Why don't you sit down?" He motioned to a bench next to the wall.

Ochus quickly handed the baby back to Mary and sat on the dilapidated bench.

"Mary and I were pledged to be married," Joseph said, taking a deep breath, "but then she was found to be with child." He paused. "It's not what you think, though. It was to fulfill another scripture—that a virgin would be with child and would give birth to a son."[14]

A virgin having a baby?

"Mary is that virgin."

"But that's impossible," Thorn said.

"Well," Joseph went on, "the prophecy also says that he'd be called Immanuel. It means 'God with us.'[15] God, you see, put a piece of Himself inside of Mary. This baby is not from man. He's from God. He *is* God. He's come to deliver us from our sins."

God? Ochus thought.

"The only way our Lord could save us," Joseph said, "was to become one of us."

Ochus abruptly stood. *This is crazy. How could God be a baby?*

"Excuse me, please." He scrambled to the door. "I need some air."

How long had he heard about the Hebrew God? How often had the Jews talked about His righteousness and redemption?

Now, how can I be standing in front of Him? In front of God? The Jewish God is holy, isn't He? Ochus glanced back at the house as he walked through a nearby field. *How could He be born in such a lowly place, only to be surrounded by stargazers?*

"Are you lost?" a burly voice called from behind him.

Ochus turned to see a man holding a shivering lamb.

"Uh, no," Ochus said, glancing at a fire-lit cave just paces away. "I'm here visiting a king. His name is Jesus. He was born under the star."

"Actually He was born right here in this cave," the man said. He balanced the lamb in one hand and grabbed Ochus with the other, pulling him toward the cavern. Ochus stared at a body lying at the entrance, stretched from one side of the cutout door to the other.

"Don't worry about him," the man said, stepping over the body. "A shepherd always sleeps in the doorway of a cave. It's only right that he puts himself between his flock and savage animals."[16]

The man gently placed the quivering lamb on its feet.

A stench of animal dung stung Ochus's nose as he

watched the lamb run to the back of the cave.

"I found the lamb," the shepherd called to a few men sitting around the fire. "That little guy wandered all the way to the other side of Bethlehem."

They nodded and then once again talked among themselves.

"This is where I first saw the baby," the shepherd said to Ochus. He sat down next to a small feeding-trough and dangled his fingers above the dried stalks of wheat.

"In this manger?" Ochus dropped to his knees and stared at the clay box.

"It might as well have been His throne," the shepherd said. "He never cried or fussed. He was perfectly content being among the fodder that feeds the sheep."

This God was born in a stable? Ochus thought, looking to the top of the cave. Rings of smoke drifted up to it, becoming a part of the thick, black soot.

"But how did the King get here?" Ochus asked.

"Mary and Joseph traveled here from Nazareth up north," the shepherd said. "You know, for the census that Caesar commanded."

He pulled out a dirty cloth and wiped the bloody cuts on his hands. "When they got to Bethlehem, there was nowhere for them to stay. So they came here to this sheepfold."

"Surely, someone would have made room for the King," Ochus said.

"Well, I guess someone finally did," the shepherd said. "They're now staying in that guest house. They've been there for awhile."

But do people understand He's God? Ochus thought.

"Hardly anyone knows He's the Messiah," the shepherd

said as he pushed himself to his feet. "We've told some people. But we plan to go into the big city tomorrow and spread the word — to tell everyone what the angel told us."

The shepherd paused and then cupped his hands around his mouth.

"Today in the town of David," he shouted, "a Savior has been born to you. He's Christ the Lord."[17]

The Lord? Ochus thought, feeling his heart race. *He's really the Lord.*

"I'd better go check on the sheep," the shepherd said, pointing to the rear of the cave. "You don't mind showing yourself out, do you?"

Ochus didn't answer as he scrambled to the entrance. He couldn't wait to get back and hold the baby — to hold God.

"A Savior has been born to you," he could hear the shepherd shout again as he ran toward the house. "He's Christ the Lord."

By the time Ochus got there, the windows were dark. The camels were tethered close by.

Zara and the others must still be inside.

How could they fall asleep with God in the room? Didn't they want to ask questions? Didn't they want to know more about Him? There were so many things he would ask.

I'll just have to wait till morning, he thought, sitting down next to the door and closing his eyes.

❧

"Hurry, hurry, move it!" Thorn said in a loud whisper.

Ochus felt someone stumble over his leg.

"What's going on?" He scrambled to his feet.

"We're getting out of here," Thorn said, running to his camel.

"All of us had a dream," Cyrus said as he walked up and put his hand on Ochus's shoulder. "We were commanded to not go back to Herod's palace, but to return to Persia by another route."

"I told you Herod was crazy," Thorn said.

"We're leaving," Cyrus continued.

Ochus stepped back. "But we can't leave God."

"You're as crazy as they are," Thorn yelled, climbing onto his camel. "You either come with us now or you stay here."

Cyrus nudged him, motioning toward the camels.

"But I can't go," Ochus said. "Don't you see? This God is actually alive."

"If you won't come," Zara said, kicking his camel, "we must leave without you—assistant or not."

Ochus nodded.

"Take care of yourself," Cyrus called as they hurried down the road.

Ochus watched them disappear into a valley and then slowly sat back on the ground.

"I'll never leave God," he whispered.

❧

Before the sun could rise, Mary stepped out of the house, holding baby Jesus.

"We're going to Egypt," she said as Joseph loaded a small bag onto a donkey.

"Egypt?" Ochus questioned. "Well then, I'll go, too."

"No, it's not safe for you to come," Mary said. "Herod is looking for Jesus, and he'll stop at nothing to kill him."

She placed the baby in his arms. This time, just for a moment.

"Don't ever forget Him," she said.

The next day hundreds of people came looking for the King. The shepherds had shouted His arrival in the streets of Jerusalem just as they had promised.

Ochus hung his head as he passed Herod's soldiers.

"Where's the Jewish king?" one of them asked. He shrugged like he'd seen so many others do.

❧

Later he heard that the soldiers had killed every male infant in Bethlehem, searching for the Jewish Savior.

Everyone thought Jesus had died that morning. But Ochus knew He was alive and would one day return.

He never went back to Persia. The green valley outside Jerusalem became his home. For years, he worked in the olive groves, making rich, green oil. And always, he kept watch for Jesus. Eavesdropping on people's conversations, he waited to hear news about Mary, Joseph, and the Messiah.

"There's a man preaching in Capernaum who claims to be the Son of God," a coworker commented one day from the other side of an olive tree.

Ochus could hardly believe his ears. He stopped picking and climbed down the ladder. He had another journey to make.

"Joseph son of David,
do not be afraid to take
Mary home as your wife,
because what is
conceived in her is
from the Holy Spirit.
She will give birth to *a
son,* and you are to give
him the name *Jesus,*
because he will *save his
people from their sins."*

MATTHEW 1:20-21

A Second Look at
The Child

Prophecy

I see him, but not now; I behold him, but not near. A star will come out of Jacob; a scepter will rise out of Israel. (Numbers 24:17)

> #### *Fulfillment*
> *He will be great and will be called the Son of the Most High . . . He will reign over the house of Jacob forever. (Luke 1:32-33)*

Prophecy

The scepter will not depart from Judah, nor the ruler's staff from between his feet, until he comes to whom it belongs and the obedience of the nations is his. (Genesis 49:10)

> #### *Fulfillment*
> *For it is clear that our Lord descended from Judah. (Hebrews 7:14)*

Prophecy

"The days are coming," declares the LORD, "when I will raise up to David a righteous Branch, a King who will reign wisely and do what is just and right in the land." (Jeremiah 23:5)

Fulfillment
Remember Jesus Christ, raised from the dead,
descended from David. This is my gospel.
(2 Timothy 2:8)

PROPHECY
But you, Bethlehem Ephrathah, though you are small
among the clans of Judah, out of you will come for me
one who will be ruler over Israel, whose origins are from
old, from ancient times. (Micah 5:2)

Fulfillment
So Joseph also went up from the town of
Nazareth in Galilee to Judea, to Bethlehem . . .
He went there to register with Mary . . . While
they were there, the time came for the baby to be
born. (Luke 2:4-6)

PROPHECY
For to us a child is born, to us a son is given, and the
government will be on his shoulders. And he will be
called Wonderful Counselor, Mighty God, Everlasting
Father, Prince of Peace. (Isaiah 9:6)

Fulfillment
"For God so loved the world that he gave his one
and only Son, that whoever believes in him shall
not perish but have eternal life." (John 3:16)

PROPHECY
"Therefore the Lord himself will give you a sign: The virgin will be with child and will give birth to a son, and will call him Immanuel." (Isaiah 7:14)

> *Fulfillment*
> *"How will this be," Mary asked the angel, "since I am a virgin?" The angel answered, "The Holy Spirit will come upon you, and the power of the Most High will overshadow you. So the holy one to be born will be called the Son of God." (Luke 1:34-35)*

PROPHECY
Out of Egypt I called my son. (Hosea 11:1)

> *Fulfillment*
> *An angel of the Lord appeared to Joseph in a dream . . . "take the child and his mother and escape to Egypt." . . . After Herod died, an angel of the Lord appeared in a dream to Joseph in Egypt and said, . . . "take the child and his mother and go to the land of Israel, for those who were trying to take the child's life are dead." (Matthew 2:13,19-20)*

∞

Witness the birth of Jesus and travel with the magi as they journey to worship the newborn King:

Matthew 1–2
Luke 1:26-38; 2:1-20

CHAPTER TEN

THE DWELLING PLACE

Jesus in the Temple

Clement stared as the morning light cut across Judas's face. It moved over his left eye and down his cheek, leaving the rest of his body in darkness.

"Twenty-eight, twenty-nine, thirty," Clement finished counting, spinning the silver shekels across the marble table.

They clattered into Judas's outstretched hand. He counted them one by one.

"Don't you trust a priest?" Clement said. "After all, I am the temple's chief treasurer."

Laughter echoed through the chamber. But it wasn't a joke.

"This money," he announced, "is going for a good cause. I know our treasury is meant for buying lambs and goats, but this is just as important as any sin sacrifice."

He stared at the others sitting around the room.

"Jesus will do more for us than any offering. With his blood, we'll all be better off."

He grabbed Judas's arm and pulled him to his feet.

"So, you'll watch and tell us when it's best to capture Jesus."

Judas stuffed the jingling coins under his sash.

"Well then, I'll walk you to the temple's main gate." Clement turned toward the council. "We're done with this part of the meeting," he said as he led Judas out the door.

As usual, the temple's colonnade was empty. Only a few priests passed on their way to the morning service.

"This way," Clement said, glancing at Judas's knotted hair.

Who would have thought that such a lowly character would bring the Sanhedrin together? After all, the Pharisees and Sadducees had so little in common. The pious Jews rarely mixed with power-hungry chief priests.[1]

But now, Clement thought, *we finally agree on something.* Even if it was murder.

"Well," he said as they stopped in front of the hovering archway, "when you return, ask for me."

Judas nodded and then scurried through the gate.

What a fool. Who would betray a friend for only thirty pieces of silver?

But what did Clement care how cheaply the traitor

worked? Soon, no one would follow Jesus. The priests
would once again be the only religious authority.

"So," a voice called as Clement stepped into the Court
of Priests, "is it all settled?"

Clement twisted around. Caiaphas, the high priest,
stood on the other side of the baluster.

"It is," Clement said.

Caiaphas smiled and ran his fingers through his gray
beard. "You're in charge of the lamps this week." He strutted to the altar.

Lamps? Clement thought. *Who could think about lamps
at a time like this?*

"Shouldn't I keep an eye on Judas?"

"It's your job to care for the temple. And don't worry—
Judas will deliver the goods soon enough."

Well, I suppose I can hurry through my duties, Clement
thought. He walked to the cleansing basin and dunked his
hands into the water.

Surely, his skin was clean enough. But he always had
to wash it before going into the sanctuary. It was God's
command.

That should be sufficient, he figured, wiping his hands on
his robe.

He climbed the sweeping stairs and stepped through the
sanctuary's door. Turning toward the lampstand, he tripped
on a stone that protruded from the base of the wall.

"That silly stone," he cursed.

How many times had he stumbled on the cornerstone?
Countless, he thought, limping to the lampstand.

He ran his fingers over the gold branches and then over
the carved almond flowers. "Wait and watch," he muttered.

Everyone knew that almond trees were the first sign of spring. When the trees bloomed, everyone waited for the new life that would follow.[2]

But what life are we waiting for? Clement shook his head.

It was useless to think about. Who could understand all of God's explicit instructions?

Like the bread. Clement looked across the room at the twelve unleavened loaves stacked on top of a wide table. Why was it there?

And what about the incense at the front of the room? Clement looked up at the smoke rising to the roof.

Even priests can't understand the meaning of it all, he thought as he cut the lamp's wicks and lit each one with the middle flame.

"Finally, it's done," he said as the last one burned.

The sanctuary always made him nervous. *After all, God is behind there,* he thought, glancing at the thick curtain hanging at the front of the Holy Place.

Behind the veil was a room called the Holy of Holies, or the Most Holy Place. In the wilderness that's where God had hovered over the ark of the covenant.

Clement imagined the ornate box with its thick slab of gold resting on top. He could almost see the carved cherubim staring down at the lid.

"But now there's nothing in the room but a rock," Clement whispered.

The ark had been missing for years. Instead of sprinkling sacrificial blood on the atonement cover, the high priest now poured it onto a large stone.[3]

Clement squinted, trying to peek into the room. The

curtain had been closed for generations. No one, except the high priest, was allowed inside.

If God really cared about us, Clement thought, turning toward the door, *why would He hide inside that tiny room?*

"I'll be praying if anyone needs me," he called to a priest. But he wasn't going to pray. All he could do was think of Jesus.

What an annoying man. Clement walked to his quarters. *How can Jesus say he'd lay down his life for us? And what nerve to claim that we need to be cleansed!*

He shook his head, stepping into his room.

Jesus calls himself light and bread. But we don't need him for life! He even says he'll acknowledge us before the Lord. Clement stopped in front of a window. *Does Jesus think he's smoke or incense? How can he go to God in heaven?*

He paused and looked out at the sanctuary.

But is that enough reason to kill him?

He stared at the altar for a long time and then paced back and forth until the sun began to set.

"What am I thinking?" he said, dropping onto his mat and closing his eyes. "Of course we should kill him."

❧

The morning sun blazed through the window. Clement awoke, startled.

Judas might be here.

But he wasn't. And as the day passed, Clement grew more and more anxious walking through the temple compound's vast rooms. By the time night fell, he was pivoting in small circles, biting the tip of his thumbnail.

"Judas is back," a guard finally yelled from the other side of the dark colonnade.

"Ah, Judas," Clement called as he walked toward the silhouetted figure in the doorway. "We've been waiting for you."

He stopped and then looked back over his shoulder.

"Have the guards meet us out front," he told a man on the other side of the court. "And tell the chief priests that Judas has arrived. Oh, and request some Roman soldiers to assist us."

They'll make things look more official, he thought as he again turned to Judas.

"So tell me," he said, stepping toward the gate, "how will we know to capture Jesus? What will be your sign?"

Judas didn't answer as they walked out of the temple into the night air.

"Well," Clement said, "he's your friend, isn't he? Maybe a kiss would be appropriate."

He squinted at the outline of the temple guards waving their burning torches. A few shook thick clubs above their heads. Finally, the guards would see real conflict. Securing the sanctuary had to be painfully boring.[4]

"Judas will betray Jesus with a kiss," Clement spread the word, pausing as Roman soldiers strutted around the corner.

He looked down at one of their clubs, feeling his stomach sink. He could almost see Jesus' blood covering it.

Are we doing the right thing? he thought. *Does Jesus really deserve to die? Has he done anything so wrong?*

"I can't go," Clement abruptly said, grabbing a torch from one of the guards and handing it to Judas. "I'm needed here."

He turned to one of the chief priests.

"Tilon," he said, "report to me everything that happens."

He hurried back to the temple as the torches crackled behind him. Never looking back, he ran to the sanctuary.

I shouldn't go there, he thought. The last thing he needed was to feel more anxious. But he had to check the lamps.

He stepped through the sanctuary's door. Then once again, he stumbled on the cornerstone.

"Why do I always trip on that?" he sighed as he leaned against the wall.

He looked down at the bruises on his leg.

"See, I lay a stone in Zion," he slowly said, repeating a scripture he'd learned long ago, "a tested stone, a precious cornerstone for a sure foundation. The one who trusts will never be dismayed."[5]

But what does that mean? How can I trust in a stone?

"The Lord Almighty is the one you're to regard as holy." he whispered the words from the prophet Isaiah. "And he'll be a sanctuary. But for both houses of Israel, he'll be a stone that causes men to stumble and a rock that makes them fall."[6]

Once, he had heard Jesus talk about the stone—after Jesus had told a story of a landowner whose son was killed by a group of tenants.[7]

"The stone the builders rejected," Jesus said, "has become the capstone."[8]

Clement dropped his head.

"Am I like the tenants?" he said. "Am I rejecting the Stone? Am I killing God's Son?"

No, it can't be, he thought. He shivered as he sat on the marble floor.

"Things will look different in the morning," he told himself, looking up at the lamp's flames.

֍

"We captured Jesus," a man said as the morning rooster crowed.

Clement jerked up to see Tilon.

"We took him to Caiaphas. The entire Sanhedrin was there. And now, they've bound him and led him to Pilate."

"Really?" Clement scrambled to his feet.

"Yes," Tilon said. Red streaks ran through each of his eyes. "None of us could figure out what charges to bring against him. Then two members said they heard him proclaim he would destroy the temple and rebuild it in three days."[9]

"You twisted his words," Clement said. "He actually meant if someone *else* destroyed it, he would raise it in three days."[10]

"I know, I know," Tilon said. "Then Caiaphas asked if he was the Son of God. And get this, Jesus said yes. Can you believe that?"

The Son of God? Clement shivered at the words

"Then we started pushing and punching him," Tilon went on. "I belted him really good. You should have been there. It was brilliant."

"You really didn't have to hit him, did you?" Clement's hands were sweating as he grabbed the wall for support.

"What's wrong with you?" Tilon said. "I thought you would have taken the first punch."

Suddenly, a ringing sound echoed behind them.

Clement turned to see silver shekels bouncing against the altar. He ran down the steps, with Tilon close behind. "Judas, what are you doing?"

"I've sinned," Judas said, leaning on the railing. "I've betrayed innocent blood."[11] The disciple lunged forward, thrusting the remaining coins at Clement.

"I've betrayed Jesus," he wailed as he turned and ran from the court.

Clement watched him go and then looked back at the spinning coins.

"Thirty pieces of silver," he gasped. "I can't believe I gave Judas thirty pieces of silver."

His mouth went dry.

"And Judas actually threw them back into the temple," he said, barely able to speak. "Just like the prophecy predicts."

"What are you talking about?" Tilon said.

"You know, the prophecy from Zechariah."

Clement bent down, picking up one of the coins. "If you think it best, give me my pay. But if not, keep it. So they paid me thirty pieces of silver. And the Lord said to me, 'Throw it to the potter'—the handsome price at which they priced me! So I took the thirty pieces of silver and threw them into the house of the Lord to the potter."[12]

Clement brushed his thumb over the smooth metal.

"That means nothing," Tilon said. "You might have priced Jesus at thirty pieces of silver. But that's also the price of a slave. Think about it—is Jesus our slave? How can his life serve us?"[13]

Tilon reached out and snatched the coin from Clement's hand. "Let's just get rid of this money. We can't use it, anyway. It's blood money."

Tilon bent down and gathered the coins. "Caiaphas and I have had our eyes on a plot of land for a while. It's that field, you know, on the eastern side of the Valley of Hinnom. We could buy that."

"Yes, I know the field," Clement said. "I think it's called the potter's field."[14]

"Oh, so it is." Tilon's voice cracked. "Well then, that makes the prophecy complete, doesn't it?"

Clement nodded. His heart sank as he walked toward the sanctuary.

"Don't worry," Tilon called. "They're probably about to crucify Jesus, and then it won't matter, anyway. He'll be dead. You should be happy."

Happy? Clement thought as he walked toward the lampstand. *I've just helped kill God's Son. Who could be happy?*

Now what will happen to me? Clement cringed, thinking of God's punishment.

"Please, keep burning," he said to the lamp. He could almost hear the shouting in the distance. "You can't die. You're the Son of God."

Maybe he could run and tell the people. But it would be useless. No one would listen.

"I've stumbled over the Stone," he confessed. "We've all stumbled over Him. He's the Cornerstone. He's the center of our religion."

Wasn't every aspect of their faith based on Him coming?

"He's here," Clement said, touching the lampstand's almond flowers.

Why didn't he see it before? Why did it take him tripping over that stone to understand it?

"I'm sorry," he said.

Suddenly, he heard Jesus' voice as if it were in the sanctuary. "Father, forgive them."[15]

Forgive them? Clement thought. He must be hearing things.

"How can I be forgiven?" he shouted as the lampstand began to shake. "I'm the one who murdered you."

The cups rattled.

What's happening? Clement watched the flames tremble. The stacked loaves swayed with the table.

"It's finished," he could almost hear Jesus say.[16]

Suddenly a jagged slit ripped down the thick curtain guarding the Most Holy Place, fracturing it in two. Both sides hung limply next to each other.[17]

The curtain, he thought as the shaking stopped, *it's open.* He walked toward it and peered through the gash, touching the frayed material.

But I can't go in there. God will kill me.

He looked inside—down at the bloodstain on the rock.

"Forgiven," he gasped as he stepped into the room and fell to his knees.

Did Jesus' death bring him forgiveness? Was He God's Sacrifice?

That's crazy.

But how else could Clement be inside the room and still be alive? Only the high priest was allowed in there—and only if he came with blood.

I don't have blood. He looked at his hands. *Or do I?*

"Yes," he whispered. "I have Jesus' blood. That's why the curtain is open."

Clement turned and grabbed the torn material.

"Now, I can be in God's presence. Jesus' blood has broken the barrier."

He lifted his head and looked out into the sanctuary.

"Jesus was the Light—He showed us who God is. And He was the Bread, giving us true food."

Clement stared down at his clean hands. "He was the bloody Altar and cleansing Water that covered my sins. He was the Incense that interceded for me."

Jesus was like every piece of furniture in the temple. He *was* the Temple.

Clement glanced around the room. *The furniture,* he realized, *is set up in the shape of a cross.*

Was this God's plan all along? When He looked down at the temple, had He really been looking at His crucified Son?

But now He's dead. And what am I supposed to do without Him?

He stared at the lamps.

"Destroy this temple," he remembered Jesus' words, "and I'll raise it again in three days."

Was Jesus talking about Himself? Clement thought.

"Lord," he called into the air. "Are you going to raise Jesus? Will He live again?"

Clement had never been more confused in his life. But still, he felt a peace he could not explain, and a presence that he knew would always dwell inside him.

Don't you know
that *you* yourselves
are *God's temple*
and that
*God's Spirit lives
in you?*

Therefore, brothers, since
we have confidence to
enter the *Most Holy Place*
by the *blood of Jesus,* by
a new and living way
opened for us through the
curtain, that is, his body . . .
let us draw near to God
with a sincere heart in full
assurance of faith, having
our hearts sprinkled to
cleanse us from a guilty
conscience and having
our bodies washed
with pure water.

HEBREWS 10:19-22

A Second Look at
The Dwelling Place

Prophecy

The LORD said to Moses, ". . . Then have them make a sanctuary for me, and I will dwell among them." (Exodus 25:1,8)

> *Fulfillment*
> *The Word became flesh and made his dwelling among us. (John 1:14)*

Prophecy

Then the LORD said to Moses, "Make a bronze basin, with its bronze stand, for washing. Place it between the Tent of Meeting and the altar and put water in it. Aaron and his sons are to wash their hands and feet with water from it. Whenever they enter the Tent of Meeting, they shall wash with water so that they will not die." (Exodus 30:17-20)

> *Fulfillment*
> *But you were washed, you were sanctified, you were justified in the name of the Lord Jesus Christ and by the Spirit of our God. (1 Corinthians 6:11)*

PROPHECY

"Make a lampstand of pure gold . . . and on the lamp-stand there are to be four cups shaped like almond flowers with buds and blossoms . . . Then make its seven lamps and set them up on it so that they light the space in front of it." (Exodus 25:31,34,37)

> *Fulfillment*
> *When Jesus spoke again to the people, he said, "I am the light of the world. Whoever follows me will never walk in darkness, but will have the light of life." (John 8:12)*

PROPHECY

"Make a table of acacia wood . . . Put the bread of the Presence on this table to be before me at all times." (Exodus 25:23,30)

> *Fulfillment*
> *Then Jesus declared, "I am the bread of life. He who comes to me will never go hungry." (John 6:35)*

PROPHECY

"Make an altar of acacia wood for burning incense." (Exodus 30:1)

> *Fulfillment*
> *"Whoever acknowledges me before men, I will also acknowledge him before my Father in heaven." (Matthew 10:32)*

PROPHECY

"He shall then slaughter the goat for the sin offering for the people and take its blood behind the curtain . . . He shall sprinkle it on the atonement cover and in front of it." (Leviticus 16:15)

> *Fulfillment*
> *This is love: not that we loved God, but that he loved us and sent his Son as an atoning sacrifice for our sins. (1 John 4:10)*

PROPHECY

"Hang the curtain from the clasps and place the ark of the Testimony behind the curtain. The curtain will separate the Holy Place from the Most Holy Place." (Exodus 26:33)

> *Fulfillment*
> *And when Jesus had cried out again in a loud voice, he gave up his spirit. At that moment the curtain of the temple was torn in two from top to bottom. (Matthew 27:50-51)*
>
> *Therefore, since we have been justified through faith, we have peace with God through our Lord Jesus Christ, through whom we have gained access by faith into this grace in which we now stand. (Romans 5:1-2)*

PROPHECY

I told them, "If you think it best, give me my pay; but if not, keep it." So they paid me thirty pieces of silver. And the LORD said to me, "Throw it to the potter"—the handsome price at which they priced me! So I took the thirty pieces of silver and threw them into the house of the LORD to the potter. (Zechariah 11:12-13)

> *Fulfillment*
> *When Judas, who had betrayed him, saw that Jesus was condemned, he was seized with remorse and returned the thirty silver coins to the chief priests and the elders . . . The chief priests picked up the coins and said, "It is against the law to put this into the treasury, since it is blood money." So they decided to use the money to buy the potter's field as a burial place for foreigners. (Matthew 27:3,6-7)*

∞

I pray that out of his glorious riches . . .

> "If anyone loves me . . . my Father will love him, and we will come to him and make our home with him."
> JOHN 14:23

. . . Christ may dwell in your hearts. (Ephesians 3:16-17)

Consequently, you are . . . members of God's household, built on the foundation of the apostles and prophets, with Christ Jesus himself as the chief cornerstone. In him the whole building is joined

together and rises to become a holy temple in the
Lord. And in him you too are being built together
to become a dwelling in which God lives by his
Spirit.

EPHESIANS 2:19-22

∞

Study the Dwelling Place as it transforms from a building
and becomes our hearts:

Exodus 25–27; 30 — Instructions for Building the
Tabernacle/Temple

Matthew 26:57-68; 27:1-10,32-54 — The Trial and
Crucifixion of Jesus

CHAPTER ELEVEN

THE KING

*Jesus in the Kingdom Prophecies
and in Psalm 22*

Beno squeezed the melon before pulling it up to his nose and sniffing its sweet scent.

"Perfect," he said to himself as he covertly dropped it into his large leather sack and shoved his way to the other side of the busy fruit stand.

Looks like these were picked today, he thought, grabbing a plum and pressing his finger into its tender skin. *The fresher the better.*

He looked around at the clamoring shoppers. Then he rolled three of the largest plums into his open bag.

Sure, he was choosy about his fruit. But why shouldn't he be?

You can never be too picky about pillage. Why steal what nobody else wants?

He winked at the oblivious merchant and turned from the fruit stand.

I've got the quickest hands in Jerusalem, he thought, racing up the road toward a crowd gathered on the winding path.

"What's going on here?" he said to no one in particular.

But he really didn't care. It only mattered that there was a crowd. What thief could resist a large gathering?

He scurried ahead and pushed toward the center of the action, spotting several open satchels. Quickly, he reached for a man's pouch.

But just as he did, the man yanked his sash from his waist and flung his coat into the road.

Beno stumbled back.

"Hosanna," the people began to chant. "Save us now."

Hosanna? Why are they shouting for God's deliverance?[1]

"Here," an old man yelled, shoving a palm branch into his hand. "You'll need one of these."

Beno glanced down at the flimsy twig.

"The Branch," the man said, motioning out to the road, "has arrived."

Beno looked up and spotted a donkey weaving its way down the road, through the scattered palm fronds and robes. Two skinny feet dangled from each side, almost dragging on the bumpy ground.

"Rejoice greatly, O Daughter of Zion!" the old man yelled. "Shout, Daughter of Jerusalem! See, your King comes to you, righteous and having salvation, gentle and riding on a donkey."[2]

Beno hadn't heard that prophecy in years. But how could he forget it? As a boy he memorized the whole thing, dreaming of a messiah—a king—who would come to save Israel.

"That's our King," the man proclaimed. "That's our Branch."

Beno lurched forward

It couldn't be. He stared at the man perched on the tiny animal. His shoulders were slumped and his head hung, bobbing with the rhythm of the donkey.

"That's no king," Beno shouted.

"Sure it is," the man said. "He's gentle and rides a donkey—just like the prophecy says."

But I always imagined a larger donkey, Beno thought, *almost like a white horse. Not a pitiful gray one. And what about the rest of the prophecy?*

After all, it said that the king would rule to the ends of the earth.[3]

Beno stared again at the donkey's rider. *Does that look like someone who'll rule the earth?*

Many prophecies, though, told of both a victorious ruler and a meek savior.

How can one person be both? Beno thought. *How can a king ride a donkey and rule the whole earth?*

It was too confusing to think about. Maybe that's why he so rarely went to synagogue. Who wanted a weak savior? Beno robbed weak people. A cowardly messiah could never save anyone.

"Jesus," the old man said, "says that His kingdom is at hand."

Jesus? Beno thought. *Oh, so this is that Jesus character.*

He'd often heard of him during his trips up north, when he went to steal from rich people.

"How absurd," Beno said. "He doesn't even have a crown."

"Don't worry," the man answered. "Soon He'll have one."

But he can't even afford the clothes on his back, Beno thought. *And what about an army? Doesn't a king need an army?*

Beno shook his head as Jesus bounced past him.

"Blessed is the coming kingdom of our father David," the man yelled. "Blessed is the King of Israel!"[4]

He waved his palm branch in the air. Its leaves whipped back and forth, blowing Beno's hair off his face.

"It's like the prophet Jeremiah said," the man called as he walked forward. "The Lord will raise up to David a righteous Branch, a King who will reign wisely."[5]

Beno didn't move.

"Jesus is from the line of David," the man said. "He *is* the Branch. He *is* the King."

Beno squeezed the rough branch in his hand. "Jesus isn't the mighty branch." He dropped the sprig onto the ground.

They're all crazy, he thought, cutting between the masses of people. Finally, he turned and watched the mob move past him toward the temple.

Jesus isn't the Savior. What a waste of time. I didn't even steal one thing.

"Excuse me," someone said. He felt a hand press into his back.

His heart pounded as he spun around. He hated when people sneaked up behind him.

A woman with no expression stumbled past him. *Oh, it's just a blind person,* he thought.

He watched the woman walk all the way to the temple and bump into its outside wall. Slowly, she guided herself into the main gate.

"Coming through. Coming through," a man yelled.

Beno quickly stepped to the side. Three men carrying a cot rushed past him.

"We've got a sick boy here," one of them shouted. "We're looking for Jesus."

They can't be serious, Beno thought as he watched them scramble under the temple's archway. *Jesus is a fake. He's just a poor, weak man.*

"Someone should stop him," Beno whispered, hurrying toward the temple.

Surely, the priests would do it. After all, Jesus had gone too far.

Beno turned the corner and walked under the temple's eastern stairs.

"Heal her!" someone yelled.

He looked up at the outer court. Jesus held his hands over the blind woman's face, covering her eyes with his thumbs.

The woman stared straight ahead and then fell forward, crying as she wrapped her arms around his neck.

"She can see!" a man yelled.

Beno looked around at the cheering crowd and then again at the woman. *I don't believe it.*

"It's a hoax," a few people shouted.

Beno pushed past them, trying to get to the woman as she walked down the stairs. *There's no way she can see,* he thought. She was blind. He had seen it himself. By the time he managed to elbow by several onlookers, he had lost her in the crowd.

This can't be happening. He looked back at Jesus.

Several priests now encircled him.

*It's just a trick. There's no use thinking about it. Soon Jesus'
real identity will be exposed. Then everyone will know the
truth.*

He glanced up to the fading sun.

It's too late to take my usual trip up north, he thought. *But
who would leave at a time like this, anyway?* Stealing would
be easy with everyone distracted by a supposed savior.

What a perfect time to take advantage of their empty houses.

Besides, he had to be back by the end of the week.
That's when his friend was scheduled to be crucified.

Beno's hands began to sweat just thinking about it. If
only his friend had taken his advice, then he would have
never been caught. Even though he was burly and over-
weight, he could have outrun the soldiers. His form of rob-
bery was just risky and clumsy—a dangerous combination.

"Someday you're going to get caught," Beno would
often tell him. "Then, you'll get the cross."

Every criminal, unless he was a Roman citizen, was in
danger of the grueling punishment.[6] The pain was excruci-
ating, and the humiliation was sometimes worse.

I should be there, Beno thought. It was only right for his
friend to see a familiar face when he died.

⁂

And so for the next four days, Beno scouted the most vul-
nerable homes, taking as much money and jewelry as his
big bag would hold. He never went to the temple or listened to Jesus. Who could bother when there was so much
money to gain?

By the end of the week, he'd stolen as much as he usually

did in a month. Finally, early in the morning, he sat in his one-room home and counted his newfound earnings.

"It's all paying off," he muttered, running his fingers through the pile of coins.

He grabbed a handful and stood.

"If Jesus wants an army," he said, laughing, "I'll gladly buy it for him."

He drizzled the coins onto the silver heap and listened to them ring.

I wish I could steal more, he thought as he turned and walked out the door. *If only I didn't have to go to Golgotha.*

A slight breeze blew dust over his feet as he crossed several streets. He cut through a long field and then climbed a dry, weedy hill. At the top, he shivered as he stared down at the place every criminal feared.

"I can't go," he murmured, gazing at the three holes dug into the crusty ground. They were just wide enough to hold the stumps of crude crosses.

He took a deep breath.

"Well," he said as he slowly walked down the hill, "I just won't get too close."

Golgotha was no place for a criminal.

He pushed his hair from his eyes and looked down the path leading from the city. A man stumbled up it. A long whip tore through the air and into his back.

That's him, Beno thought. He could tell by the man's size that it was his friend.

A small crowd trailed behind, having followed him from the prison.

Beno watched his friend stagger to one of the pits, tripping over it and tumbling to the ground. The tiny crowd cheered. Three guards threw a heavy cross onto the dirt.

I can't watch, Beno thought, looking down.

He cringed as he listened to metal hitting metal and the sound of a high-pitched shriek. Finally, the pounding stopped. But just when Beno looked up, the hammer once again swung into the air. His stomach turned as it slammed down onto his friend's hand.

"I wish you a quick death," Beno whispered.

Five soldiers grabbed the cross and pushed it up straight. It teetered as it sunk into the hole.

Suddenly, Beno saw another criminal stumble in front of the cross. Then, once again, he heard the rhythm of the pounding hammer. Screams echoed from the wood.

Good, Beno thought, eyeing the third hole. *Only two executions today.*

But just then he heard more screaming.

"Oh no," he said, looking at a mob moving up the path. "There's another one."

Several guards walked backward, trying to hold the shouting people. In front of them was a single soldier. He strutted forward and snapped his whip. A bloody man staggered ahead of him.

Who could it be? Beno thought.

He knew most of the criminals in prison. But this man was too disfigured. He was soaked in blood. A soldier shoved him toward the middle hole.

Beno quickly stepped back as the people filled in around him, pushing and shoving.

"Crucify him," a boy called. "Crucify Jesus!"

Jesus? Beno thought, jerking as he watched the third cross finally fling forward.

Beno stared at the crown of twisted sticks digging into Jesus' head.

He's wearing a crown, he thought, noting the charges scribbled on the cross.

"This is Jesus," he said, reading the large words. "The King of the Jews."

His heart raced.

"But Jesus isn't the king," he yelled. "He can't die with that title. People might think it's true."

Yet there was no use screaming. No one could hear him over the shouts and wailing of the crowd. And besides, who would take down the sign now? Every criminal had to have a charge written on his cross. How else could onlookers know what he did wrong?

This can't be happening. Jesus can't be called the king.

He looked at his friend gasping for air and then back to Jesus.

But surely people will forget, he thought. *I mean, once Jesus is dead and buried no one will even remember.*

"He trusts in God," the crowd began to chant. "Let God rescue him."[7]

Beno smiled. "Yes, let God rescue him," he yelled.

The Lord would never rescue a pitiful, fake messiah.

❧

Throughout the morning, Jesus continually pushed himself up and then slumped back down again. Now Beno could almost see his bones shift and pull as the weight of his body hung on them.

His strength is failing, Beno thought.

The meager breeze couldn't comfort Jesus' thirst and exhaustion. It only made the dust twirl beneath the cross, climbing toward him as if begging for his body.

"Death will soon take him," Beno concluded. "And then we'll all be happy."

He could see everything from where he stood. Chief priests. Jewish elders. Family and friends. A Roman soldier walked around Jesus, tugging on the nails that pierced his feet.

Don't worry, Beno thought. *He's not coming off that cross.*

The soldier nudged Jesus' body. Jesus twitched. An outline of his ribs poked through his skin. The soldier laughed, kicking a red-stained tunic toward some other guards, then sat down next to them.

Oh, the dogs are going to play some games, Beno thought as they began casting lots for the ripped pieces of the clothing.

He liked calling them dogs. Most Jews did. It was a perfect nickname for the hated Gentiles.[8]

"My God," a voice suddenly called from one of the crosses. It was Jesus. He coughed blood and then gasped, "My God, why have you forsaken me?"[9]

"He's calling on the Lord," someone shouted.

Beno caught his breath and then looked to the ground.

"My God, my God," he repeated Jesus' words, "why have you forsaken me?"

It was the first sentence of the psalm he'd always feared. Any criminal—or sinner—should shudder at the mere mention of it. After all, it told of what God would do to those He'd forsaken.

Beno had memorized most of it. How could he not?

Someday, it would be his fate.

"My God, my God, why have you forsaken me?" Beno said.

He looked up and continued with the psalm. "I am a worm and not a man, scorned by men and despised by people. All who see me mock me. They hurl insults, shaking their heads: 'He trusts in the Lord. Let the Lord rescue him.'"[10]

Beno stared at Jesus.

"I am poured out like water, and all my bones are out of joint. My strength is dried up like a potsherd, and my tongue sticks to the roof of my mouth. You lay me down in the dust of death."[11]

He glanced at the soldiers, still playing their game.

"Dogs have surrounded me," he continued. "A band of evil men has encircled me, they have pierced my hands and my feet. I can count all of my bones. People stare and gloat over me. They divide my garments among them and cast lots for my clothing."[12]

Beno jolted back in recognition.

What's going on? he thought. *It's just as the psalm said it would be!*

"Jesus," a voice suddenly called.

Beno looked up at the crosses.

"Remember me," his friend shouted, "when you come into your kingdom."[13]

Kingdom? Beno thought

Jesus dropped his head and then pulled it up again. "Today," he said, "you'll be with me in paradise."[14]

My friend, in paradise? Beno thought. *That can never happen. How can Jesus say that?*

He felt a hand grab onto his arm.

"It's not a beautiful crown," a voice said. "But still, it's a crown."

Beno turned. The old man he had met the other day was standing next to him.

"My name is Rosh," he said. "I don't think we were properly introduced."

Beno didn't respond.

"I saw you drop your branch. I suppose you don't believe Jesus is the King." Rosh leaned forward. "My God, my God," he slowly said, "why have you forsaken me?"

Beno's body quivered as he stepped back.

"Oh, so you're familiar with that psalm?" Rosh said. "Well, then you know it speaks of exactly what's going on here."

Beno couldn't deny it. He saw the similarities. But how could he explain it?

"Jesus is the Messiah," Rosh said. "And that psalm, written a thousand years ago, is a prophecy about Him. He's being forsaken so that we'll never be."[15]

Beno watched Jesus, still heaving and gasping for air.

"But why is he being forsaken?"

"It's simple, really. The answer is found in the same psalm. It says that He's doing it to fulfill two vows—a vow to buy an army of souls and a vow to build a kingdom."

"An army?" Beno whispered. "And a kingdom?"

"Yes, the psalm says that after the Lord delivers His life from the power of the dogs and the horns of the bulls, Jesus will fulfill those vows."[16]

Rosh motioned toward Beno's friend.

"It says that those who seek the Lord will live forever.[17]

That sinner up there will now live forever. His soul is being
purchased. Jesus is buying it with His life."

Can that really be? Beno thought as Rosh grabbed his
arm and leaned closer.

"In Zechariah it says that the Branch will remove the sin
of this land in a single day."[18] Rosh paused. "Jesus is removing the sin of that thief—and of all people. He's removing
sin from our land."[19]

Even from me? Beno thought.

"If you believe it," Rosh said, "Jesus will remove your
sins. Your heart will live forever in paradise."

Rosh took a deep breath. "The rest of the psalm says
that all the ends of the earth will remember and turn to the
Lord. And all the nations will bow down before Him. He
will rule over everyone."[20]

Rosh looked up at Jesus. "It will be a mighty kingdom,"
he said.

Beno felt his head whirl. "But if he's really the Messiah,
Jesus could build his kingdom now. I mean, he could have
ridden into Jerusalem on a white horse, not a donkey."

The old man smiled. "Jesus has to be a suffering Servant
in order to be a mighty Ruler. Don't you see? He's come
now in humility to purchase His army, His saints—to buy
them with His blood. And then He'll return in power and
glory, bringing His army with Him. He'll rule forever."

With power and glory? Beno thought.

"You have a choice," Rosh said. "You can be on either
side of Jesus' cross. You can be the sinner who's called Him
King—the one who's now been purchased. Or you can be
the one who's mocked Him and ignored Him—the one
who will be shut out of paradise."[21]

Rosh paused and then continued. "Jesus has fulfilled His first vow. He's been forsaken for your soul. Don't be fooled; He'll fulfill His second vow. He'll come back to rule."

Rosh rested his hand on Beno's shoulder as he turned to leave. "It's your choice," he said.

Beno stared at the crosses. He looked at his dying friend and then at the other criminal.

I don't want to be forsaken. I want to belong to the army.

Out of the corner of his eye he saw a small palm branch on the ground, obviously discarded at the victory parade just a few days before.

The Branch, he whispered as he knelt down and retrieved it.

Standing, he waved it triumphantly above his head. "Blessed is the kingdom of our father David," he shouted, looking at Jesus.

He glanced over at Rosh, now starting up the road.

"Blessed is the Branch," he yelled. "He is the Messiah. He is the King."

Jesus answered,
"You are right in saying I
am *a king.* In fact, for
this reason *I was born,*
and for this *I came
into the world.*"

JOHN 18:37

207

A Second Look at
The King

Prophecy

Rejoice greatly, O Daughter of Zion! Shout, Daughter of
Jerusalem! See, your king comes to you, righteous and
having salvation, gentle and riding on a donkey, on a colt,
the foal of a donkey. (Zechariah 9:9)

Fulfillment
*When they brought the colt to Jesus and threw
their cloaks over it, he sat on it. Many people
spread their cloaks on the road, while others
spread branches they had cut in the fields. Those
who went ahead and those who followed shouted, "Hosanna!" "Blessed is he who comes in the
name of the Lord!" "Blessed is the coming kingdom of our father David!" (Mark 11:7-10)*

Prophecy

"The days are coming," declares the LORD, "when I will
raise up to David a righteous Branch, a King who will
reign wisely and do what is just and right in the land."
(Jeremiah 23:5)

Fulfillment
*"[Jesus] will be great and will be called the Son
of the Most High. The Lord God will give him
the throne of his father David, and he will reign*

*over the house of Jacob forever; his kingdom will
never end." (Luke 1:32-33)*

PROPHECY
My God, my God, why have you forsaken me?
(Psalm 22:1)

> *Fulfillment*
> *About the ninth hour Jesus cried out in a loud
> voice, "Eloi, Eloi, lama sabachthani?"—which
> means, "My God, my God, why have you for-
> saken me?" (Matthew 27:46)*

PROPHECY
But I am a worm and not a man, scorned by men and
despised by the people. All who see me mock me; they
hurl insults, shaking their heads: "He trusts in the LORD;
let the LORD rescue him." (Psalm 22:6-8)

> *Fulfillment*
> *Those who passed by hurled insults at him,
> shaking their heads . . . In the same way the
> chief priests, the teachers of the law and the
> elders mocked him. "He saved others," they
> said, "but he can't save himself . . . He trusts
> in God. Let God rescue him." (Matthew
> 27:39,41-43)*

PROPHECY
Dogs have surrounded me; a band of evil men has encir-
cled me, they have pierced my hands and my feet.
(Psalm 22:16)

Fulfillment
So the soldiers took charge of Jesus . . . he went out to the place of the Skull. Here, they crucified him. (John 19:16-18)

PROPHECY
They divide my garments among them and cast lots for my clothing. (Psalm 22:18)

Fulfillment
When the soldiers crucified Jesus, they took his clothes, dividing them into four shares, one for each of them, with the undergarment remaining . . . "Let's not tear it," they said to one another. "Let's decide by lot who will get it." This happened that the scripture might be fulfilled. (John 19:23-24)

PROPHECY
From you comes the theme of my praise in the great assembly; before those who fear you will I fulfill my vows. The poor will eat and be satisfied; they who seek the LORD will praise him — may your hearts live forever! (Psalm 22:25-26)

Fulfillment
For the Lord himself will come down from heaven, with a loud command, with the voice of the archangel and with the trumpet call of God, and the dead in Christ will rise first. After that, we who are still alive and are left will be caught up together with them in the clouds to meet the Lord

in the air. And so we will be with the Lord forever.
(1 Thessalonians 4:16-17)

PROPHECY
All the ends of the earth will remember and turn to the
LORD, and all the families of the nations will bow down
before him, for dominion belongs to the LORD and he
rules over the nations. (Psalm 22:27-28)

> *Fulfillment*
> *"At that time the sign of the Son of Man will*
> *appear in the sky, and all the nations of the*
> *earth will mourn. They will see the Son of Man*
> *coming on the clouds of the sky, with power and*
> *great glory. And he will send his angels with a*
> *loud trumpet call, and they will gather his elect*
> *from the four winds, from one end of the heav-*
> *ens to the other." (Matthew 24:30-31)*

PROPHECY
"I am going to bring my servant, the Branch . . . and I
will remove the sin of this land in a single day."
(Zechariah 3:8,9)

> *Fulfillment*
> *But you know that he appeared so that he might*
> *take away our sins. (1 John 3:5)*

For to be sure, he was crucified in weakness, . . .

But we see Jesus, who was made a little lower than the angels, now crowned with glory and honor because he suffered death.

HEBREWS 2:9

I looked and there before me was a great multitude that no one could count, from every nation, tribe, people and language, standing before the throne and in front of the Lamb. They were wearing white robes and were holding palm branches in their hands. And they cried out in a loud voice: "Salvation belongs to our God, who sits on the throne."

REVELATION 7:9-10

. . . yet he lives by God's power. (2 Corinthians 13:4)

I saw heaven standing open and there before me was a white horse, whose rider is called Faithful and True. With justice he judges and makes war. His eyes are like blazing fire, and on his head are many crowns. He has a name written on him that no one knows but he himself. He is dressed in a robe dipped in blood, and his name is the Word of God. The armies of heaven were following him, riding on white horses and dressed in fine linen, white and clean. Out of his mouth comes a sharp sword with which to strike down the nations. "He will rule them with an iron scepter." . . . On his robe and on his thigh he has this name written: KING OF KINGS AND LORD OF LORDS.

REVELATION 19:11-16

"See, the Lord is coming with thousands upon thousands of his holy ones."

JUDE 14

Therefore, since we are receiving a kingdom that cannot be shaken, let us be thankful, and so worship God acceptably with reverence and awe.

HEBREWS 12:28

He who testifies to these things says, "Yes, I am coming soon." Amen. Come, Lord Jesus.

REVELATION 22:20

∞

Experience Jesus' triumphal entry by reading Luke 19:28-48. And see the prophetic fulfillment of the King on the cross in Psalm 22 and Matthew 27:27-50.

GOD'S STORY

"For I tell you the truth," Jesus once said to His disciples, "many prophets and righteous men have longed to see what you see but did not see it, and to hear what you hear but did not hear it."[1]

See what? His disciples might have thought. *What did the prophets long to see?*

I would have asked the same question.

What about you?

What about now? Have you seen what the prophets longed to see? Have you heard what their ears burned to hear?

Surely, you've listened to the shouts of the crucified Lamb on the cross. You've heard the cry of Eve's Seed in Bethlehem. You've seen Canaan. You've bowed to the King, and you've tasted God's Bread.

"Blessed are your eyes because they see," Jesus said, "and your ears because they hear."[2]

We're blessed because we see Jesus as God's Messiah. We recognize Him as the fulfillment of Old Testament prophecies.

That's what Jesus wanted.

And that's what the writers of the New Testament wanted. They packed the Scriptures full of examples, arguments, and reflections of Old Testament prophecies. I'm convinced that one of the main reasons—if not *the* reason—they wrote the letters of the New Testament was to show how Jesus fulfilled the messianic prophecies.

But were the apostles' explanations their own ideas? Did the predictions of the prophets originate from their own knowledge?

Sure, the Bible seems to have been written by human effort. Moses wrote the first five books. David, Solomon, and the prophets wrote much of the rest of the Old Testament. The disciples and apostles compiled the New Testament. Over a period of fifteen hundred years, more than forty different people wrote the Bible's sixty-six books.[3]

Yet, whether they explained creation or the conquering of Canaan, it didn't matter. From beginning to end, they all proclaimed the same message of redemption.

But how? How could their words have had so much unity?

Could it be that the Bible really wasn't written by people? Maybe it had just one Author.

"For prophecy never had its origin in the will of man," the Bible says, "but men spoke from God as they were carried along by the Holy Spirit."[4]

Through the Holy Spirit, God wrote His plan of salvation. He scribbled it on the hearts of the prophets, and He revealed it in the hearts of the apostles. Just as the Old Testament speaks of a Christ who's coming, the New Testament proclaims a Christ who's already come.

The Bible was written by one Author, telling one Story.

And God wrote it in the most creative way. He hid His message of redemption within the adventures of His ancient people. Their lives had double meanings. Their experiences were multidimensional.

Through the words of Moses, God told the story of Adam and Eve's disobedience and their eventual covering with animal skins. On another level, this saga pictures our sinful state being covered with the ultimate Sacrifice. And still, it goes even deeper, telling of how one day we'll be given new, heavenly bodies.

Again through Moses, God chronicled the building of the tabernacle. Its candlestick, bread table, and Holy of Holies were all described precisely. But within these instructions was an exact picture of Jesus, who now tabernacles in our hearts. Soon, the Mighty Temple will again dwell among us.

God is the only One who could have written these predictions.

He's the only One who knows the future.

In Psalm 22, when King David foresaw the Messiah pierced through His hands and feet, death by crucifixion was basically unknown. Jews never practiced it. They stoned their criminals. It wasn't until the Romans perfected the cross that the execution style became widely popular.[5]

How could David, hundreds of years before the Roman cross, have predicted that the Messiah would have been pinned to it?

He couldn't have. Only the Lord knew that.

God alone wrote His Salvation Story. A story that's so simple a child can understand it, but so complex many will spend their lives trying to grasp it.

Jesus is the only man in history who fulfilled the exact details of God's creative Saga. Scholars calculate that the chances of this are literally a quadrillion to one.[6]

A skeptic's common explanation is that the Scriptures have been changed over the years. In order to discount God's amazing Story, people hang on to the frail belief that the Bible has been rewritten through time. But evidence abounds that the Scriptures are very much the same as they were thousands of years ago.

Between 1947 and 1956, archaeologists discovered dozens of ancient scrolls in the caves of Qumran along Israel's Dead Sea. These documents, otherwise known as the Dead Sea Scrolls, were written by a sect of Jews much like the Pharisees. Among various books of the Bible, a complete copy of Isaiah was found. Scholars date it to have been written around 125 B.C.[7]

Until that discovery, the oldest known book of Isaiah was composed in A.D. 900. With careful examination of the two copies—with one thousand years passing between them—it was determined that very little had changed. Of the 166 words in Isaiah 53, only one word was in question, and that word did not change the meaning of the chapter.[8]

Scholars don't know the exact dates that the Old Testament was written. But they do know that it was translated from Hebrew into Greek around 250 B.C. It's only logical to assume that it had to have been completed in order to have been translated. Therefore, most historians agree that the Old Testament was finished at least two hundred years before the birth of Jesus.[9]

This means the Scriptures could *not* have been changed

to fit Christ's life. Rather, His life fulfilled them.

It seems that history proves the Scriptures are sturdy and strong.

Like most of Jesus' early followers, I'm not a scholar or even an intellectual. But I can read a story. I can feel its ink sink into my soul, changing me forever. I can grasp that God wrote the Bible. His stories are living—moving through time—and we won't see their final conclusion until Jesus returns.

"It's easier," Christ said, "for heaven and earth to disappear than for the least stroke of a pen to drop out of the Law."[10]

The Bible is true and alive. It has the power to change us and reside inside our hearts—to meet us in our every situation, calming us in our fears and teaching us in our shortcomings.

But it's also the Light before the Son. It's a portrait of Jesus—allowing people to identify Him thousands of years before He was born and helping us to recognize what the prophets longed to see and hear.

The Bible is truly the living Word.

It's God's Salvation Story.

And we have the *word of the prophets* made more certain, and you will do well to *pay attention to it,* as to a *light shining in a dark place,* until the day dawns and the morning star rises in your hearts.

2 PETER 1:19

A SECOND LOOK AT
God's Story

I am saying nothing beyond . . .

> Concerning this salvation, the prophets, who spoke of the grace that was to come to you, searched intently and with the greatest care, trying to find out the time and circumstances to which the Spirit of Christ in them was pointing when he predicted the sufferings of Christ and the glories that would follow. It was revealed to them that they were not serving themselves but you, when they spoke of the things that have now been told you by those who have preached the gospel to you by the Holy Spirit sent from heaven.
>
> 1 PETER 1:10-12

. . . what the prophets and Moses said would happen. (Acts 26:22)

> "I am the Alpha and the Omega," says the Lord God, "who is, and who was, and who is to come, the Almighty."
>
> REVELATION 1:8

BIBLIOGRAPHY

Booker, Richard. *The Miracle of the Scarlet Thread.* Shippensburg, PA: Destiny Image Publishers, 1981.

Brown, William. *The Tabernacle: Its Priests and Its Services.* Peabody, MA: Hendrickson Publishers, 1996.

De Haan, M. R. II. *God's House of Symbols: A Walk Through the Old Testament Tabernacle.* Grand Rapids, MI: RBC Ministries, 1981.

Edersheim, Alfred. *The Life and Times of Jesus the Messiah.* Peabody, MA: Hendrickson Publishers, 1993.

Edersheim, Alfred. *The Temple: Its Ministry and Services.* Peabody, MA: Hendrickson Publishers, 1994.

Graham, Billy. *The Holy Spirit.* Nashville: Word, 1988.

Habershon, Ada R. *Study of the Types.* Grand Rapids, MI: Kregel Publications, 1997.

Henry, Matthew. *Matthew Henry's Commentary on the Whole Bible.* Peabody, MA: Hendrickson Publishers, 1991.

Howard, Kevin, and Rosenthal, Marvin. *The Feasts of the Lord.* Nashville: Nelson, 1997.

LaHaye, Tim. *Jesus: Who Is He?* Sisters, OR: Questar Publishers, 1996.

Lockyer, Herbert. *All the Messianic Prophecies of the Bible.* Grand Rapids, MI: Zondervan, 1973.

Lockyer, Herbert, ed. *Illustrated Dictionary of the Bible.* Nashville: Nelson, 1986.

MacDonald, William, ed. *Believer's Bible Commentary.* Nashville: Nelson, 1990.

McDowell, Josh, and Stewart, Don. *Answers to Tough Questions Skeptics Ask About the Christian Faith.* Wheaton, IL: Tyndale, 1980.

McDowell, Josh. *Evidence That Demands a Verdict.* Nashville: Nelson, 1979.

McGee, J. Vernon. *Thru The Bible Commentary Series— Acts Chapters 1–14.* Nashville: Nelson, 1991.

McGee, J. Vernon. *Thru The Bible Commentary Series— Isaiah Chapters 1–35.* Nashville: Nelson, 1991.

McGee, J. Vernon. *Thru The Bible Commentary Series— Leviticus Chapters 1–14.* Nashville: Nelson, 1991.

Mears, Henrietta C. *What the Bible Is All About.* Wheaton, IL: Tyndale, 1987.

Muncaster, Ralph O. *Can You Trust the Bible?* Eugene, OR: Harvest House, 2000.

Packer, J. I., and Tenney, M. C., eds. *Illustrated Manners and Customs of the Bible.* Nashville: Nelson, 1980.

Richards, Larry. *Every Covenant and Promise in the Bible.* Nashville: Nelson, 1998.

Rosen, Moishe. *Y'shua: The Jewish Way to Say Jesus.* Chicago: Moody, 1982.

Simpson, A. B. *The Christ in the Bible Commentary, vol 1.* Camp Hill, PA: Christian Publications, 1992.

Simpson, A. B. *Christ in the Tabernacle.* Camp Hill, PA: Christian Publications, 1985.

Thomas, W. Ian, Major. *The Saving Life of Christ.* Grand Rapids, MI: Zondervan, 1961.

NOTES

INTRODUCTION: ON THE ROAD

1. Luke 24:17 (paraphrased).

2. Luke 24:18 (paraphrased).

3. Luke 24:20-24 (paraphrased).

4. Luke 24:25 (paraphrased).

5. Luke 24:26.

6. Luke 24:27 (paraphrased).

7. Tim LaHaye, *Jesus: Who Is He?* (Sisters, OR: Questar Publishers, 1996), p. 176.

8. LaHaye, pp. 173-174.

9. John 5:39-40.

10. Luke 4:18-19.

11. Luke 4:21.

12. Acts 17:2-3.

13. Acts 17:11.

CHAPTER ONE: THE LAMB

1. Herbert Lockyer, ed., *Illustrated Dictionary of the Bible* (Nashville: Nelson, 1986), p. 267.

2. John 19:31.

3. Exodus 12:46.

4. Exodus 12:9.

5. Exodus 12:10.

6. Exodus 12:5.

7. Exodus 12:3,6.

8. From Psalm 34:19-20,22.

9. John 1:29.

10. John 19:33-34.

CHAPTER TWO:
THE BURIED BREAD AND RISEN FRUIT
1. Herbert Lockyer, ed., *Illustrated Dictionary of the Bible* (Nashville: Nelson, 1986), p. 473.

2. Lockyer, p. 473.

3. John 6:51.

4. From John 6:51.

5. Kevin Howard and Marvin Rosenthal, *The Feasts of the Lord* (Nashville: Nelson, 1997), p. 68-69.

6. Lockyer, p.152.

CHAPTER THREE: THE NEW GRAIN
1. Isaiah 49:6.

2. Acts 2:15.

3. From Acts 2:22-23.

4. From Acts 2:24.

5. From Acts 2:32-33.

6. Acts 2:38 (paraphrased).

7. Acts 10:1-8.

8. Acts 10:28.

9. Acts 10:34-36.

10. From Acts 10:36,43.

11. John 12:23-24.

CHAPTER FOUR: THE SEED

1. Genesis 3:22-23.

2. Genesis 3:2-6.

3. Genesis 3:24.

4. Genesis 3:15 (paraphrased).

5. Genesis 4:1.

6. Genesis 3:20.

7. Genesis 3:15 (paraphrased).

8. Genesis 12:1,4.

9. Genesis 12:10-20.

10. Genesis 15:1-6.

11. William MacDonald, *Believer's Bible Commentary* (Nashville: Nelson, 1990), p. 1691.

CHAPTER FIVE: THE NEW COVENANT

1. From Exodus 24:8.

2. Exodus 24:9-11.

3. From Luke 22:20.

4. From Jeremiah 31:31-32.

5. Jeremiah 31:33,34.

6. From Luke 22:42.

7. From Luke 22:42.

CHAPTER SIX: THE WEARY'S REST

1. Numbers 13:26–14:4.

2. Numbers 14:19-35.

3. Deuteronomy 3:20; 12:10.

4. Deuteronomy 12:10; Numbers 13:21-28.

5. Deuteronomy 12:8-9 (paraphrased).

6. Joshua 2:24 (paraphrased).

7. Joshua 2:8-13.

8. Hebrews 3:5.

9. Hebrews 3:7-9 (paraphrased).

10. From Hebrews 3:10-11.

11. Hebrews 3:12,14.

12. Hebrews 3:19 (paraphrased).

13. From Hebrews 4:1.

14. From Hebrews 4:8-10.

15. Hebrews 4:11.

16. From Matthew 11:28-30.

Chapter Seven:
The Priest and the Offering
1. Leviticus 17:11.

2. Hebrews 8:5.

3. Richard Booker, *The Miracle of the Scarlet Thread*
(Shippensburg, PA: Destiny Image Publishers,
1981), pp. 91-92.

4. From Psalm 40:5.

5. From Psalm 40:6.

6. Psalm 40:6.

7. Exodus 21:5-6.

8. From Psalm 40:6-7.

9. From Psalm 110:4.

10. Genesis 14:17-20.

11. Hebrews 6:20–7:27.

12. Psalm 110:1,4.

Chapter Eight: The Refuge
1. From Luke 23:34.

2. Numbers 35:15.

3. Isaiah 53:12 and Isaiah 52:10.

4. Isaiah 53:2-3.

5. Isaiah 53:4-5.

6. Isaiah 53:7-9 (paraphrased).

7. Isaiah 53:10-11 (paraphrased).

CHAPTER NINE: THE CHILD

1. Herbert Lockyer, ed., *Illustrated Dictionary of the Bible* (Nashville: Nelson, 1986), p. 1104.

2. Lockyer, p. 1104.

3. Numbers 24:17.

4. Genesis 49:10.

5. Jeremiah 23:5.

6. Lockyer, p. 476.

7. From Matthew 2:3-6, which quotes Micah 5:2.

8. Matthew 2:8 (paraphrased).

9. From Isaiah 9:6.

10. Daniel 2:1-3,24.

11. Lockyer, p. 556.

12. Matthew 1:21.

13. Matthew 1:1-16.

14. Isaiah 7:14.

15. Lockyer, p. 503.

16. Lockyer, pp. 979-980.

17. From Luke 2:11.

CHAPTER TEN: THE DWELLING PLACE

1. Herbert Lockyer, ed., *Illustrated Dictionary of the Bible* (Nashville: Nelson, 1986), pp. 936, 950.

2. M. R. De Haan II, *God's House of Symbols: A Walk Through the Old Testament Tabernacle* (Grand Rapids, MI: RBC Ministries, 1981), p. 6.

3. Alfred Edersheim, *The Temple: Its Ministry and Services* (Peabody, MA: Hendrickson Publishers, 1994), p. 34.

4. Edersheim, p. 61.

5. Isaiah 28:16.

6. From Isaiah 8:13-14.

7. Matthew 21:33-40.

8. Matthew 21:42 and Psalm 118:22.

9. Matthew 26:61.

10. John 2:19.

11. From Matthew 27:4.

12. From Zechariah 11:12-13.

13. William MacDonald, *Believer's Bible Commentary* (Nashville: Nelson, 1990), p. 1167.

14. Matthew 27:6-10; Lockyer, p. 862.

15. Luke 23:34.

16. From John 19:30.

17. Matthew 27:50-51.

CHAPTER ELEVEN: THE KING

1. Herbert Lockyer, ed., *Illustrated Dictionary of the Bible* (Nashville: Nelson, 1986), p. 490.

2. From Zechariah 9:9.

3. Zechariah 9:10.

4. Mark 11:10 and John 12:13.

5. Jeremiah 23:5 (paraphrased).

6. Lockyer, p. 267.

7. Matthew 27:43.

8. William MacDonald, *Believer's Bible Commentary* (Nashville: Nelson, 1990), p. 578.

9. Psalm 22:1; Matthew 27:46.

10. From Psalm 22:6-8.

11. From Psalm 22:14-15.

12. From Psalm 22:16-18.

13. Luke 23:42.

14. From Luke 23:43.

15. MacDonald, p. 577.

16. Psalm 22:20-21,25.

17. Psalm 22:26.

18. Zechariah 3:8-9.

19. Matthew Henry, *Matthew Henry's Commentary on the Whole Bible* (Peabody, MA: Hendrickson Publishers, 1991), p. 1573.

20. Psalm 22:27-28 (paraphrased).

21. MacDonald, p. 1456.

CONCLUSION: GOD'S STORY

1. Matthew 13:17.

2. Matthew 13:16.

3. Josh McDowell and Don Stewart, *Answers to Tough Questions Skeptics Ask About the Christian Faith* (Wheaton, IL: Tyndale, 1980), p. 18.

4. 2 Peter 1:21.

5. Moishe Rosen, *Y'shua: The Jewish Way to Say Jesus* (Chicago: Moody, 1982), p. 45.

6. Tim LaHaye, *Jesus: Who Is He?* (Sisters, OR: Questar Publishers, 1996), p. 178.

7. Josh McDowell, *Evidence that Demands a Verdict* (Nashville: Nelson, 1979), p. 58.

8. McDowell, p. 58.

9. McDowell, p. 144.

10. Luke 16:17.

ABOUT THE AUTHOR

For Julianna Treadwell, to write is to worship. Her favorite form of praising the Lord comes with a pen and paper. Her written words have graced many greeting cards as well as radio airwaves and newspaper pages. Julianna is inquisitive at heart and loves to travel. While journeying through Israel, she began to explore Old Testament prophecies. Much of what she learned is in this book. If you'd like to contact Julianna, she can be reached at www.Julianna Treadwell.com.

SEE THE BIBLE IN A NEW LIGHT.

The Divine Intruder

Jim Edwards creatively retells Bible stories in a way
that shows us clearly how powerfully God's
involvement in our lives impacts us.
(James R. Edwards)

The Pursuit of Holiness

Holiness should mark the life of every Christian. But holiness
is often hard to understand. Learn what holiness is and
how to say "no" to the things that hinder it.
(Jerry Bridges)

The Message: New Testament with Psalms and Proverbs

Written in easy-to-understand, contemporary language, Eugene
Peterson tells the stories of the biblical past in a way that
makes them come uniquely alive in the present.
(Eugene H. Peterson)

Get your copies today at your local bookstore, visit our web-
site at www.navpress.com, or call (800) 366-7788 and ask for
offer #BPA or a FREE catalog of NavPress products.